I0420717

SECURITY SECTOR REFORM:
A CASE STUDY APPROACH TO TRANSITION
AND CAPACITY BUILDING

Sarah Meharg
Aleisha Arnusch

Susan Merrill
Editor

January 2010

Originally published by the Strategic Studies Institute .

*****

Comments pertaining to this report are invited and should be
forwarded to: Director, Strategic Studies Institute, U.S. Army War
College, 122 Forbes Ave, Carlisle, PA 17013-5244.

*****

PKSOI's website address is *https://pksoi.army.mil.*

*****

FOREWORD

Security sector reform (SSR)—defined here as activities undertaken by a nation and its partners to improve the way it provides safety, security, and justice to its citizens—has emerged since the end of the Cold War as an important tool for stabilizing and reconstructing post-conflict countries. It is a particularly important tool in the context of failing or failed states, offering a means of arresting the failure process in the first instance and supporting failed state recovery in the second. The U.S. Government endorses the concept of SSR as a component of stabilization and reconstruction with the devotion of an entire chapter to the subject in the new (October 2008) U.S. Army *Field Manual* 3-07, *Stability Operations.*

In this paper, the authors explore the definition of SSR as it has emerged in the international community, including the United States, its bilateral partners, and various intergovernmental organizations. It examines the makeup of the security sector, identifies emergent principles for implementing SSR in the community of practice, and specifies the outcomes that SSR is designed to produce. The supporting case studies of Haiti, Liberia, and Kosovo assess the impact of SSR programs on host nation security sectors. The authors conclude that those conducting SSR programs must understand and continually revisit the policy goals of SSR programs in order to develop concepts that support a transitional process that moves forward over time. Intermediate objectives are required in support of this transition that can also articulate what is good enough and fair enough at various stages in the transformational process. State actors must acknowledge and often accommodate nonstate security actors more effectively in SSR planning and implementation, while recognizing both the advantages and the risks of collaborating with such actors. The authors also identify a need for rebalancing resources committed to SSR, especially given that justice and civil law enforcement typically are badly under-resourced as elements of SSR programs. Finally, the authors note the need for more flexible and better integrated funding processes to support SSR activities within the U.S. Government.

The Peacekeeping and Stability Operations Institute is pleased to offer this monograph as part of the ongoing debate on global and regional stability and security.

JOHN A. KARDOS
Colonel, U.S. Army Director
Peacekeeping and Stability
 Operations Institute

DOUGLAS C. LOVELACE, JR.
Director
Strategic Studies Institute

ABOUT THE CONTRIBUTORS

SARAH MEHARG is the Senior Research Associate in the Department of Research, Education, and Learning Development at the Pearson Peacekeeping Centre and Adjunct Professor at the Royal Military College of Canada. She has a regional focus on the Balkans, Afghanistan, and Iraq and is currently researching military geography and identicide and is measuring the effectiveness of reconstruction activities during peace operations. She serves as a research fellow with the Centre for Security and Defence Studies and the Canadian Defence and Foreign Affairs Institute. Dr. Meharg has published numerous articles and chapters, including two books: *Helping Hands and Loaded Arms: Navigating the Military and Humanitarian Space* (Cornwallis, Nova Scotia: Canadian Peacekeepers Press, 2007), and *Measuring What Matters in Peace Operations and Crisis Management* (Kingston, Ontario: McGill-Queen's University Press, 2009).

ALEISHA ARNUSCH has been a Research Analyst at the Pearson Peacekeeping Centre since 2006 and is currently the Lead Researcher on the Rule of Law. In 2008, she worked as a Civilian Advisor to the NATO International Security Assistance Force Headquarters in Afghanistan. Ms. Arnusch has been a consultant with NATO since 2007 on civil-military issues and worked in the United States, Portugal, Turkey, and the Netherlands on NATO courses, exercises, strategic assessments, and special projects. She has conducted conflict risk assessments, developed course curriculums, facilitated courses, helped mediate conflicts, managed a journal, and led research projects. Ms. Arnusch holds an MA (with distinction) from the

Norman Paterson School of International Affairs at Carleton University, with a focus on conflict analysis. She also holds two BA degrees (with honors) in international relations and psychology.

SUSAN MERRILL is adjunct professor at Brigham Young University. Her previous assignments included Senior Governance Advisor at the U.S. Peacekeeping and Stability Operations Institute (PKSOI), U.S Army War College (USAWC). As a senior official with the U.S. Agency for International Development (USAID), she had extensive experience in conflict and post-conflict countries in Latin America, Asia, and Africa. She has served in El Salvador, Liberia, Nicaragua, and Cambodia, as well as Bosnia and Iraq. Ms. Merrill was the first USAID representative to the USAWC and PKSOI in 2005. In 2002-03, she was selected to lead a USAID-wide task force that produced the report *Foreign Aid in the National Interest*, an examination of the successes and failures of foreign aid and the role of aid in U.S. foreign policy. In her overseas assignments, she was Acting Mission Director, Cambodia, and held senior level positions in missions in El Salvador, Liberia, Nicaragua, and Cambodia. She is an expert in post-conflict reconstruction and governance, conflict prevention and mitigation, and economic stabilization and recovery.

INTRODUCTION:
A PRIMER TO SECURITY SECTOR REFORM

Failing and failed states are not able to provide equitable safety, security, and justice to their people through the traditional state mechanisms of police, judiciary, courts, and penitentiaries. In such situations, state mechanisms are ineffective, predatory, or absent.[1] Security sector reform, commonly referred to as SSR, emerged as an activity in the 1990s in recognition of the changing international security environment and the limitations of reform approaches among interveners working in failing and failed states.[2] SSR is a relatively new discipline in the context of peace and stability operations, whether these operations are United Nations (UN)-led or otherwise managed and supported. The coherence of strategies is improving, but the 1990s and 2000s have been witness to unsustainable and inconsistent security sector reforms in places like Kosovo, Liberia, and Haiti, among others.[3] As time passes, the meta-narratives of legitimacy, accountability, efficiency, and effectiveness influence SSR activities within the international community of states involved with such reforms.

This type of reform is multisector, multilateral, multifunctional, and multidonor in nature, similar to other lines of operation in security, governance and participation, humanitarian assistance and social well-being, economic stabilization and infrastructure, and justice and reconciliation. There is no one way to conduct SSR in post-conflict environments; and the various groups, organizations, and nations involved in SSR understand it based on their own policies, doctrines, and practices. As the environment in which interventions occur becomes more complex, so too must SSR in response to these changes. The SSR lens is not a comprehensive one, and SSR approaches vary greatly within the international community, as do meanings, definitions, policies, guidance, and implementation.

Within the international community there have been successful attempts to standardize and integrate SSR through "combined funding mechanisms and enhanced collaboration among defense and development agencies."[4] Of particular note are the efforts by the Organization for Economic Cooperation and Development (OECD) and the UN. Most members of the international community use the progress achieved by the OECD and the UN, among others, to inform their own national efforts regarding this type of reform in international interventions. The standards and guidance provided through their research can be found in country policies in Canada, the United Kingdom (UK), and the United States, as well as international processes at the North Atlantic Treaty Organization (NATO) and other international organizations. This is a significant step forward in improving the approach to reform and allowing for local capacities in host nations to be a part of such reforms. The notion that the West can intervene in places like Kosovo, Timor Leste, Liberia, and Haiti through a sort of neo-colonialism meted out through westernized policies and programs is nearly expunged from the imagination of the international community. A far better and more broadly accepted approach is to convene with host nations to build their own capacities to legitimize and sustain reform over the long haul. This paradigm shift permits the international community to move from perpetual leadership into a role of mentorship that enables a cleaner transition towards an exit strategy.

The international community, however, remains on the upswing of the learning curve related to SSR. Many approaches have been attempted since the conflicts in the early 1990s in the former Yugoslavia. Nations have endeavored to sort out their policies and procedures for SSR as they are integrating their approaches to international interventions. Not only are nations joining up their governmental responses by collocating defense, diplomacy, development, justice, policing, and corrections in mission planning, nations also continue to intervene together in multinational integrated operations. Whether a particular nation takes the lead in such an operation is irrelevant, as the integrated process forces the international community to work together to advance the global peace and security agenda.

Generally, SSR is understood as the set of policies, plans, programs, and activities that are undertaken by a series of stakeholders to improve the way a state or governing body provides safety, security, and justice to its civilian population within the context of *rule of law*. Rule of law is the principle under which all persons, institutions, and entities (both public and private), as well as the state itself, are accountable to laws that are publicly spread, enforced, and independently arbitrated consistent with international human rights law and other international standards.[5] According to U.S. Government documents, the desired outcome of SSR programs is an effective and legitimate security sector that is firmly rooted within the rule of law.

SSR attempts to build capacities within the intricate network of institutional instruments that can positively affect public safety and the rule of law. The security sector includes those organs of government with which the power of coercive authority can execute the will of the state. Understandably, such coercive power, if used

3

inappropriately, can have long-term negative effects on a state and its people. Reforms address the ways in which such power is applied and through which mechanisms. Mechanisms can be state actors as well as nonstate actors that challenge the state through force. In this respect, an insurgent, warlord, or crime boss is as much a part of the security sector as the police force, military, judiciary, and legislature.[6]

Reforms aim to provide an effective and legitimate public service that is transparent, accountable to civil authority, and responsive to the needs of the public. They may include integrated activities to support defense and armed forces reform; civilian management and oversight; justice, police, corrections, and intelligence reform; national security planning and strategy support; border management; disarmament, demobilization, and reintegration (DDR); and concurrent reduction of armed violence, especially after contemporary armed conflict.[7]

SSR is also called *security system reform*. This reframing came about with the understanding that security is an integrated activity within a system of state and nonstate systems, which include not only the armed forces, police, gendarmerie, intelligence services, justice, and penal systems, but also the civil authorities responsible for oversight and democratic control (e.g., parliament, the executive, and the defense ministry).[8] The term *security system* is used to emphasize the interconnectivity of its numerous components. This reframing was spearheaded by the OECD, while the United States and the UN have maintained the term *sector* when referring to the SSR agenda. The acronym SSR encompasses both frameworks.

SECURITY SECTOR REFORM AGENDAS

United Nations.

The UN policies that focus on maintaining and promoting peace and security are closely related to the SSR agenda. UN major policy and operational areas for supporting SSR are through peacekeeping and post-conflict peacebuilding missions and activities. Peacekeeping missions have both implicit and explicit responsibilities to SSR, most particularly in the civilian police reforms. The UN also upholds that SSR is an essential component for any stabilization process. UN efforts in transitioning countries are relevant to SSR as evidenced by the importance the UN places on the DDR of former combatants. UN policies related to the broader development agenda — the protection of human rights, gender equality, and the promotion of the rule of law and democracy — are also SSR-relevant areas.[9]

Organization for Economic Cooperation and Development.

The members of the OECD view development and security as inextricably linked. This agenda treats security in partner countries as a public policy and governance issue, inviting greater public scrutiny of security policy. Security concerns not only emphasize stability but also the safety and well-being of people. Security in all its dimensions is fundamental to reducing poverty, protecting human rights, and achieving UN Millennium Development Goals (MDGs). According to the OECD, the SSR agenda seeks to increase the ability of partner countries to meet the range of security needs within their societies in a manner consistent with democratic norms and sound principles of governance, transparency, and the rule of law. A democratic, legitimate, accountable, and efficient security system reduces the risk of violent conflict.[10]

European Union.

Although the threat of open conflict in southeastern Europe has declined, according to the member states of the European Union (EU), an effective SSR agenda across the region remains critical. Unreformed security institutions can obstruct the progress of reform, block regional cooperation, and hence undermine stability. Effective, efficient, legitimate, and accountable SSR is a prerequisite for potential accession to the EU and NATO. As the countries in this region are hinged upon one another for various reasons, SSR failure in Kosovo can have direct implications for security in the others, and vice versa.[11]

United Kingdom Government.

The UK Government's Global Conflict Prevention Pool (GCPP) defines SSR as a broad concept that covers a wide spectrum of disciplines, actors, and activities. SSR addresses security-related policy, legislation, structure, and oversight issues, all set within recognized democratic norms and principles.[12]

A review of these international community SSR agendas makes clear that there are some common tenets related to success, including effectiveness, efficiency, legitimacy, and accountability. The SSR agenda favors a holistic approach to include most aspects of the security sector, including nonmilitary ones. In other words, SSR must be comprehensive and integrated to maximize the capacities of the sectors involved to shape the environment sufficiently for sustainable success over the long term. SSR is a normative concept in that SSR is intended to increase the efficiency, effectiveness, legitimacy, and accountability of state security mechanisms, but also to improve the governance of the security sector in accordance with democratic standards. SSR is a multipurpose concept that is context-specific. Commitment to SSR is long term and requires substantial resources to achieve the sustainable outcomes that the international community is committed to.[13]

U.S. Government.

The U.S. SSR agenda is aligned with the agendas of the UN, OECD, and the EU, which contributes to an overall cohesive SSR strategy within the international community. The U.S. *National Security Strategy* (2006) suggests that the goal of U.S. statecraft is to contribute to a world of legitimate, effectively governed states that provide for the needs of their citizens and conduct activities responsibly within the international system. SSR can assist in achieving these objectives.[14] According to the U.S. Army's *Field Manual* (FM) 3-07, *Stability Operations* (2008), SSR is an activity that can reinforce diplomatic and defense interventions while reducing long-term security threats by building capacities for stable, prosperous, and peaceful societies. SSR facilitates security cooperation, capacity-building activities, stability operations, and engagement. Finally, SSR builds on the U.S. tradition of working in partnership with foreign governments and organizations to support peace, security, and effective governance.[15] SSR in countries of key national interest support U.S. foreign policy objectives.

According to FM 3-07, SSR involves reestablishing or reforming institutions and key ministerial positions that maintain and provide oversight for the safety and security of the host nation and its people. Through unified action, those individuals and institutions assume an effective, legitimate, and accountable role: they provide external and internal security for their citizens under the civilian control of a legitimate state authority. Effective SSR enables a state to build its capacity to provide security and justice. SSR promotes stability, fosters reform processes, and enables economic development. The desired outcome of SSR programs is an effective and legitimate security sector firmly rooted within the rule of law.[16]

SSR includes efforts targeting the individuals and institutions that provide a nation's security as well as promote and strengthen the rule of law. By recognizing the inherently interdependent aspects of the security sector and by integrating operational support with institutional reform and governance, SSR promotes effective, legitimate, transparent, and accountable security and justice. SSR captures the full range of security activities under the broad umbrella of a single, coherent framework. It spans from military and police training to weapons destruction and from community security to DDR of former combatants to security sector oversight and budgeting.[17]

As the United States considers peacekeeping and peace operations as an alternate mechanism for intervention, the SSR agenda can find equal purchase within the international community of states involved with these types of post-conflict interventions. UN peacekeeping operations can be an effective means of containing conflict and resolving disputes in support of U.S. national interests. Acting in this way to support U.S. interests through the UN allows the United States to share the risks and costs of dealing with international crises with other nations. Deployment of UN peacekeeping operations, and selective U.S. participation in them, is an important tool for advancing U.S. interests and leadership.[18]

Peacekeeping is intended to separate adversaries, maintain internationally and national agreed-to cease-fires, facilitate the delivery of humanitarian relief, help create conditions where refugees and displaced persons can return home, constrain the forces of opposing parties, facilitate peace talks, and create conditions conducive to political reconciliation and the conduct of free elections. Many of these activities are a part of the reform of the security sector. Peacekeeping and peace operations can help nurture new democracies, lower the global tide of refugees, reduce the likelihood of unsanctioned interventions, and prevent small conflicts from growing into larger wars. These results directly serve the national interests of the United States.[19]

PRINCIPLES OF SECURITY SECTOR REFORM

From a U.S. perspective, the key principle in successful SSR is building host nation capacities and transitioning security sector power to the ownership of the host nation. From an SSR planning perspective, it is critical to impart the notions of *capacity building, transition,* and *ownership* to the host nation institutions and the staffs of those institutions. The idea that they will eventually be taking over the reins of their interconnected sectors is a key to successful reforms.

Without this information, there may be unintended negative consequences, including a high recidivism into armed conflict and even the reestablishing of a pre-conflict status quo, which may have been a driver of the conflict in the first place.

In addition to these main principles for successful reform of the security sector, an SSR framework also needs to engage all security sector participants and meet the challenges brought about by that engagement. Inclusivity underwrites ownership. It is essential to better integrated SSR policies and greater civilian involvement and oversight. Security sector participants include state security actors, civilian police, state justice actors, nonstate providers of justice and security, sector providers of safety and security, civil society, and other nonstate actors.

State Security Actors.

This group of actors includes the traditional defense and security mechanisms of a state and those authorized by the state to use or support the use of force,[20] including military (army, navy, and air force), national police, gendarmerie, and paramilitary forces; intelligence agencies; presidential guards, coast and border guards; customs authorities; reserve or local security units; and national guard; as well as corrections and penitentiary officers.

Civilian Police.

Although national police forces can also fall under the category of state security actors, especially if there is a gendarmerie role, the regional and local police systems are often civilian police. The role of civilian police is to conduct policing at the community level through safety patrolling, investigations, and arrests, as well as to mediate local grievances and to carry out other community policing roles and responsibilities. As SSR occurs at the national level, influence over policing at the local level needs to be a part of strategic SSR planning.

State Justice Actors.

This group includes the judges that uphold the legal system legitimized by the state.

Nonstate Providers of Justice and Security.

This group includes a broad range of actors with varying degrees of legal status and legitimacy within a host nation environment. This group can include local community watch groups, militias that have been developed because of the lack of state-provided security mechanisms, paramilitary organizations, organized crime, and informal and traditional justice systems.[21]

Private Sector Providers of Safety and Security.

In the event of an intervention, it has become common for private sector companies to provide some of the security requirements in a mission. States and international organizations are turning to the private sector as a cost-effective way of procuring services that would once have been the exclusive domain of the military. *Private Military Companies* (PMCs) do not function under the same set of laws as state armed forces or UN Member State troop contributions.

PMCs are nonstate actors and are typically hired as a stop-gap measure by international organizations; nongovernmental organizations (NGOs); the UN (training, logistics, and security); nationstates that do not have standing armed forces; and states that require additional armed forces, services, and expertise to complement their standing armed forces. They perform a range of duties, including training, logistics, demining, and providing security.[22]

Civil Society.

Civil society is made up of professional organizations, civilian review boards, policy analysis organizations such as universities and think tanks, advocacy organizations, human rights commissions and ombudsman, NGOs, media, and other actors. The role of civil society in a host nation is to articulate the public demand for safety and security and to monitor security actor performance in fulfilling their role. In the event that a host nation has failed and cannot provide the security functions it normally would undertake, civil society can also fulfill functions that provide some degree of security and justice to local communities or constituents.[23]

Other Nonstate Actors.

Local nonstate actors include the general population in a conflict or post-conflict environment. Because locals are directly affected by a failed security system and weak rule of law, locals can take security and safety into their own hands. This can be done through community protection systems such as community-based patrols, curfews, and grass-roots militia development. The

12

discourse surrounding the subject of *nonstate actors* has shifted since September 2001. It is not uncommon for the term to be used by governments to veil more contentious terms such as *terrorist* and *insurgent*. The role of nonstate actors in successful SSR programs is the *transition* from local security towards state-led security mechanisms and activities that ensure the security and safety of the general population. Transition is a critical aspect of SSR planning because it reinforces the notion that states are to be responsible to their populations.

In addition to inclusivity, the principle of cooperation with and among civil authorities is critical to successful SSR planning and implementation. SSR strategies reflect a comprehensive plan that encompasses all participants in the security sector and cooperation with civil authorities.

An SSR program is based on democratic norms and underpinned by international human rights law and standards. As one of the intentions of reform of the security sector is to eliminate freedom of fear and increase human security within the civilian population of a conflict-affected country, SSR creates an environment that measurably reduces armed violence and crime. SSR enhances institutional and human capacity for security policy to function effectively and for justice to be delivered equitably so as to strengthen the rule of law.

SSR programs include well-defined policies that strengthen the governance of security institutions by establishing clear and equitable policies, accountability, and professionalism. The security sector is a part of the broader public sector and therefore must also build capacities for transparency and accountability. Programs build professional host nation security forces that are accountable to civil authorities and capable of executing their responsibilities over time and as they are capable of accepting ownership of the security sector.

It is important to note that there are a growing number of principles that contribute to successful SSR that also inform other areas of peace and stability operations. These include the principles of good governance and respect for human rights, balancing operational support with institutional reform, linking security and justice, fostering transparency between and among the host nation institutions and the interveners, and doing no harm (or doing less harm through the intervention).

As local capacities for sector reform improve and requirements for externally imposed security decrease, the principles of SSR can take hold in a host nation, along with a transition of ownership from external to internal state actors to ensure long-term sustainable development of the security sector and the rule of law.

SSR ACTIVITIES

SSR is made up of a series of standardized activities reflective of the levels of development and reforms required within a host nation's institutions (see Figure 1). Activities include the development of:

- Military Force
- Law Enforcement Force (police)
- Other Security Forces
- Border Control Forces
- Intelligence and Security Services
- Courts
- Justice
- Corrections
- Disarmament, Demobilization and Reintegration (DDR)[24]

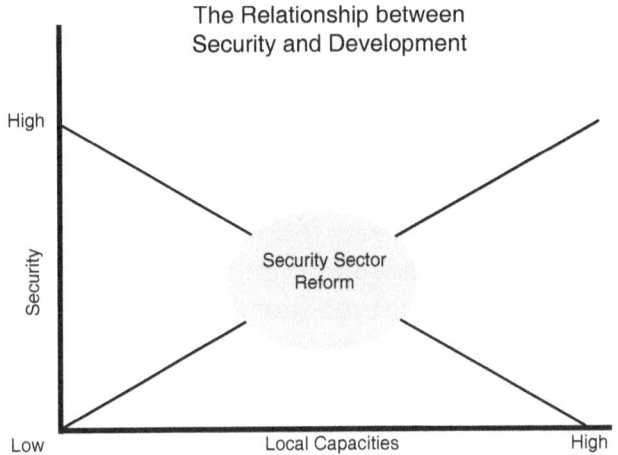

The Relationship between
Security and Development

High

Security

Security Sector
Reform

Low   Local Capacities   High

Figure 1. The Relationship between Security and Development.

These activities are interconnected in ways that are not yet fully understood by scholars, policymakers and practitioners. Moreover, it becomes critical to understand as much as possible about the security sector within a host nation so as to achieve long-term sustainable success.

OBSTACLES TO SUCCESSFUL SSR

There are many obstacles inhibiting successful SSR. SSR is interconnected with and affected by other systems, such as economics, politics, development, cultures, ideologies, geographies, histories, heritage, identities, and ethnicities. Therefore, its sustainable success is codependent on other aspects of a stability operation[25] or other type of intervention. For purposes of understanding the volatility of the security sector, it is important to understand how it can be undermined by the people and organizations of a host nation, and those beyond.

Peace spoilers are a source of risk during peace and stability operations, in particular to SSR activities. Spoilers are nonstate actors that can be individual leaders as well as organizations that believe the stability emerging from intervention threatens their power, worldview, cultural identities, and interests, and therefore they will use techniques to undermine attempts to achieve stable outcomes. These activities can include spreading rumors and fear-mongering as well as direct violence, usually against civilian populations. Spoilers are distinguished from combatants in a post-conflict environment, and can be rebels, bandits, pariahs, rogues, or terrorists.[26] Spoilers have the capacity to seriously undermine the stabilization process and can directly target interveners, which can create negative public opinion and widespread distrust. Attempts to discredit foreign interventionists (for example, the UN, NATO, and the United States) in the eyes of recipient populations are on the increase. The spoilers' intentions are to remove the threat, and this can result in increased violence in mission areas.

While spoilers are generally considered to be nonstate actors, in some mission areas experiencing the failure of state institutions, the local governments *are* essentially the organized crime networks. It is relatively easy for these nonstate actors to acquire small arms and light weapons to further their political agendas and to build armies. Often weapons obtained through legal transfers between governments end up in the hands of nonstate actors because of the corruption of governmental officials or because of the disintegration of state structures themselves.

On occasion, government-held military small arms and light weapons are distributed to nonstate actors or to the civilian population at large. These nonstate actors and their illicit trade in arms, drugs, and human trafficking complicate the stability process.[27]

In addition to local peace spoilers, diaspora populations can also have negative effects on the process of peacekeeping and peace enforcement. Diasporas often have strong communications networks within their transborder communities and can easily channel funds and weapons to their countries of origin to help their cause and undermine the SSR agenda. This is particularly problematic to interveners since the flow is often directed through legitimate and illegitimate charity organizations, which make the practice difficult to identify and to stop.

SUMMARY[28]

Reforming the security sector and strengthening the rule of law in a post-conflict host nation requires a sophisticated understanding of state and nonstate actors and the interconnectivity of such influences. There are several broad conclusions about SSR and specific recommendations for the U.S. policy community and its partners in SSR planning and implementation.

SSR stakeholders must understand and revisit the policy goals and objectives of SSR programs. Achieving a legitimate, effective, and accountable host nation security sector is aligned with the international community agenda for such reforms. To assist a host nation in realizing these types of reform, intermediate goals are required that articulate a transitional process of moving forward over time. These intermediate goals should define what is good enough and fair enough at various stages in an ongoing SSR process. This planning can consider vacillation between permissive and nonpermissive security environments in which the reforms are being implemented with the host nation. Intermediate goals must clearly address the appropriate sequencing and prioritization of SSR activities within the context of what is sustainable in terms of resourcing through the long-term commitment required for capacity building, transformation, and ownership.

There is a qualitative and functional difference between establishing security in a nonpermissive environment and providing justice and law enforcement services. Establishing security is a predominately military task, and the primary method for accomplishing that task is the defeat and detention of individuals that pose an imminent security threat to military forces and the communities that they are protecting. Establishing security in this context will not address the need for community-based justice and police services, and those implementing SSR strategies—especially at the planning stages—must recognize this issue. Transitional approaches, which blend military detention operations with longer-term programs to restore justice services and rebuild police forces, are essential. As part of a transitional approach, DDR can provide a bridge from military detention operations to a broader, community-based reconstruction process that addresses justice and police services.

There is a prevalence of nonstate security actors in the nonpermissive and semi-permissive environments where SSR is most needed. Collaboration with these nonstate actors, who frequently enjoy greater legitimacy than statutory host nation security forces within local communities, can offer significant short-term benefits to intervening forces in stability operations. Such collaboration can pose serious risks to the SSR agenda in the longer-term because some nonstate security actors tend to undermine host nation authority and are themselves prone to criminalization, abuse of human rights, and predatory behavior. SSR programs must recognize the presence of nonstate security actors in the earliest stages of planning and program design, and determine how those nonstate actors will be addressed by the SSR activities. Legitimization of such actors in the early stages can be problematic later on as authority and ownership are transitioned to a host nation.

The U.S. Government's — and U.S. partners' — efforts to conduct SSR in the justice and law enforcement areas must improve significantly. This is in part a question of out-of-balance resourcing, with too much going to defense and military activities and not enough to justice and civil law enforcement. This imbalance is exacerbated by a lack of focus at the policy level on the critical role that justice and law enforcement play in stabilization and reconstruction, and also by a lack of institutionalized best practices for capacity building and reform in the justice and law enforcement sector. Lessons learned from interventions in Haiti in the 1990s suggest that reforms of police, justice, and corrections (penitentiaries) must be likened to a three-legged stool. If one leg is weak because of under-resourcing then the stool will fall, despite the fact that one of the legs may be very strong and well-resourced. The three legs work together in a healthy security sector; one cannot be overemphasized at the peril of the others.

Efforts to address policing and law enforcement shortfalls must recognize the critical role that rule of law plays in this area, and must determine ways and means to quickly establish rule of law frameworks in transition environments. SSR stakeholders, including U.S. interagency and military actors, must address this set of gaps in capacity and capability to advance the broader U.S. SSR agenda within the agenda of the international community of partners.

Establishing an integrated funding system for SSR and crafting the necessary authorities to support that process are essential. Current U.S. Government funding processes are characterized by stovepiping and functional specialization, both in the congressional funding process and in the executive branch program design and implementation process. This fragmentation impedes efforts—both nationally and internationally—to develop integrated strategies that address sequencing and prioritizing issues across the full range of SSR activities while acknowledging the interconnectivity of the actors and institutions.

A NOTE ON THE CASE STUDIES

The case study analyses that follow this SSR primer are designed to function together. The case studies offer examples of SSR approaches in Kosovo, Liberia, and Haiti related to recommendations published in "Implementing Security Sector Reform," *Security Sector Reform Workshop, Interim Report* (Center for Naval Analyses and Peacekeeping and Stability Operations Institute, December 4, 2008), and supported by the SSR agenda outlined in the U.S. Army FM 3-07, *Stability Operations*. These two documents are listed in the Additional References section at the end of this Introduction. Each case study has a theme that complements the others, although they are not cumulative, sequential, nor comparative in their methodology.

Case Study General Outline.

1. Country Map
2. Backgrounder
3. Contemporary Context of Intervention
4. *General* and *Special* Description of SSR Activities Contextualized within the Intervention
5. Summary
6. Discussion Questions
7. Additional References and Weblinks.

ADDITIONAL REFERENCES

Publications.

Call, Charles T. ed. *Constructing Justice and Security After War* (Washington, DC: United States Institute for Peace, 2007).

Department of the Army. *Field Manual* 3-07, *Stability Operations.* Washington, DC: Headquarters, Department of the Army, October 2008. *usacac.army.mil/cac2/Repository/FM307/FM3-07.pdf.*

Dempsey, Thomas. ed. "Implementing Security Sector Reform," *Security Sector Reform Workshop, Interim Report* (Center for Naval Analyses and Peacekeeping and Stability Operations Institute, December 4, 2008). *https://pksoi.army.mil/Docs/Governance/SSR_Workshop_Interim_Report.pdf.*

Global Facilitation Network for Security Sector Reform. *A Beginner's Guide to Security Sector Reform (SSR).* March 2007. *www.peacewomen.org/resources/SSR/Gender&SSR.pdf.*

Hill, Richard, Jon Temin, and Lisa Pacholek. "Building Security Where There Is No Security," *Journal of Peacebuilding and Development*, Vol. 3, No. 2, pp. 38-52.

Rees, Edward. *Security Sector Reform (SSR) and Peace Operations: Improvisation and Confusion from the Field* (United Nations Department of Peacekeeping Operations, March 2006). *doc.operationspaix.net/serv1/MINUK_best_practices_Rees_2006-03_.pdf*.

U.S. Agency for International Development, U.S. Department of Defense, and U.S. Department of State. *Security Sector Reform*. 2009. *pdf.usaid.gov/pdf_docs/PNADN788.pdf*.

Weblinks.

Global Facilitation Network – Security Sector Reform (GFN-SSR). *www.ssrnetwork.net/*.

Organization for Economic Co-operation and Development (OECD). *www.oecd.org/*.

KOSOVO:
RULE OF LAW, POLICE, AND JUDICIARY

COUNTRY MAP

Source: Map of Kosovo, No. 4069, New York: United Nations Department of Public Information Cartographic Section, October 1998.

KOSOVO BACKGROUNDER

Until 1991, Yugoslavia was one nation comprised of six republics: Slovenia, Croatia, Bosnia Herzegovina,

Serbia, Montenegro, and Macedonia. Serbia was further divided into two autonomous regions: Kosovo and Vojvodina.

Kosovo, considered as the cultural and spiritual heart of Serbia, attained self-rule in 1974 when the Yugoslav constitution recognized the autonomous status of Kosovo, giving the province de facto self-government. Kosovo was mostly populated by Kosovar Albanians and Serbs. Pristina, the capital of Kosovo, was a modern city with a parliament, civil institutions, and other services structured to serve the people of the region.

During the Balkan wars from 1991 to 1995, Kosovo remained under the control of President Slobodan Milosevic, despite its request for independence. Milosevic's ethnic cleansing policies were turned against Kosovar Albanians so as to rid the region of non-Serbs. The Kosovar Albanians living in Kosovo responded by setting up a parallel civil adminstration, schools, and healthcare facilities. Milosevic and his politics were resisted through nonviolence in Kosovo. At this time, there were egregious human rights violations meted out against the ethnic population.

The Kosovo Liberation Army (KLA) was able to garner support from the ethnic community and proceeded with attempting to secure the civilian population against the Serb military and police. The Serb forces responded with undue force, and there were reports of massacres and indecent violations against the civilians.

Before the international interventions in Kosovo in 1999, the region represented some of the worst security sector scenarios in Europe. The public institutions in Serbia, of which Kosovo was a part, were not representative of the people of the country nor fully democratic. The rule of law — particularly in the Kosovo region — continued to break down, caused in part by a failing police, judiciary, courts, and corrections system. There was little respect for the rule of law, and the daily experience of most people was of fear and insecurity.

As attacks on ethnic groups increased, using one's language and ethnic practices became dangerous, often inciting additional violence. The economy — although not a strong one to begin with because of the failed communist economic system — was further weakened through fear, ignorance, and international sanctions against the Republic of Serbia. These sanctions included an export ban on oil sales, a ban on flights to and from Europe, and freezes on assets and travel visas. These sanctions were developed to target Serbian elites and officials aligned with Slobodan Milosevic, the former president of Serbia, who acted to further incite tensions and eventually to provoke ethnic cleansing in Kosovo against the ethnic Albanian population. The security sector of Kosovo became increasingly debilitated through intentional tactics meted out against cultures, identities, economies, ideologies, and ethnicities. Instability of systems and institutions rose considerably, further separating this region from European standards of the rule of law.

Eventually, the international community acted. First, through a negotiated cease fire brokered by U.S. special envoy Richard Holbrooke; second, by deploying 2,000 human rights observers to Kosovo under control of the Organization for Security and Cooperation in Europe (OSCE); and third, through another attempted negotiation of a peace plan in Rambouillet, France, between Serbia and Kosovo.

With the failure of successive attempts to bring a brokered peace to the region, the North Atlantic

Treaty Organization (NATO) threatened and then launched air strikes against military targets in Serbia, Montenegro, and Kosovo. The use of force by the international community prompted Milosevic to fully operationalize the ethnic cleansing of Kosovo.

"At gunpoint they forced thousands of people from their homes, burning their towns and villages afterward. Many civilians were summarily executed. Most had all their money taken, and their documents destroyed."[29] The tactics were intentional and deemed to be genocide by some members of the international community. Over 500,000 refugees fled across borders to protect themselves from the vicious attacks by the Serbian forces. As attacks against ethnic minorities increased, numbers of displaced people rose dramatically. People did not feel that the environment of their communities of origin was safe to return to, and they remained in camps or relied on the generosity of relatives in other regions. Fear, intimidation, and threat were a hindrance to returnees.

The result of such violence was the complete disintegration of the rule of law. Much of Kosovo was destroyed, as was important civilian infrastructure including bridges and oil refineries. A tenuous peace was finally brokered based on the tenets of the Rambouillet Agreement that had failed earlier.

KOSOVO TIMELINE

The following timeline provides a chronology of key events.[30]

12th century. Kosovo lies at the heart of the Serbian empire, under the Nemanjic dynasty. The period sees the building of many Serbian Orthodox churches and monasteries.

June 28, 1389. Epic Battle of Kosovo heralds 500 years of Turkish Ottoman rule. Over the ensuing decades, many Christian Serbs leave the region. Over the centuries, the religious and ethnic balance tips in favour of Muslims and Albanians.

1689-90. Austrian invasion is repelled.

1912 Balkan Wars. Serbia regains control of Kosovo from the Turks, recognized by the 1913 Treaty of London.

1918. Kosovo becomes part of the Kingdom of Serbia.

1941-World War II. Much of Kosovo becomes part of an Italian-controlled greater Albania.

1946. Kosovo is absorbed into the Yugoslav federation.

1960s. Belgrade shows increasing tolerance for Kosovan autonomy.

1974. Yugoslav constitution recognizes the autonomous status of Kosovo, giving the province de facto self-government.

1981. Troops suppress separatist rioting in the province.

1987. In a key moment in his rise to power, future president Slobodan Milosevic rallies a crowd of Kosovo Serbs, who are protesting against alleged harassment by the majority Albanian community.

1989. Yugoslav President Slobodan Milosevic proceeds to strip rights of autonomy laid down in the 1974 constitution.

July 1990. Ethnic Albanian leaders declare independence from Serbia. Belgrade dissolves the Kosovo government.

September 1990.The firing of more than 100,000 ethnic Albanian workers, including government employees and media workers, prompts general strike.

1991. Slovenia, Croatia, and Bosnia break away from Yugoslavia and declare their independence.

1992. War breaks out in the Balkans.

July 1992. An academic, Ibrahim Rugova, is elected president of the self-proclaimed Republic of Kosovo.

1993-97. Ethnic tension and armed unrest escalate.

March-September 1998. Open conflict between Serb police and separatist KLA. Serb forces launch a brutal crackdown. Civilians are driven from their homes.

September 1998. NATO gives an ultimatum to President Milosevic to halt the crackdown on Kosovo Albanians.

1998. UN Security Council Resolutions 1199 and 1203 on Kosovo.

NATO Intervention.

March 1999. Internationally-brokered peace talks fail. A crackdown by Serbs prompts NATO air raids, which are followed by massacres and an exodus of ethnic Albanians. NATO's air strikes against Yugoslavia last 78 days before Belgrade yields. Hundreds of thousands of Kosovo Albanian refugees pour into neighbouring countries, telling of massacres and forced expulsions, which followed the start of the NATO campaign.

June 1999. President Milosevic agrees to withdraw troops from Kosovo. NATO calls off air strikes. The UN sets up a Kosovo Peace Implementation Force (KFOR) and NATO forces arrive in the province. The KLA agrees to disarm. Serb civilians flee revenge attacks.

1999. UN Security Council Resolution 1244 on Kosovo.

February 2002. Rugova is elected as president by the Kosovan parliament after ethnic Albanian parties reach a power-sharing deal. Bajram Rexhepi becomes prime minister.

October 2003. First direct talks between Serbian and Kosovo Albanian leaders since 1999.

December 2003. UN sets out conditions for final status talks in 2005.

Mitrovica Clashes.

March 2004. Violence starts in the divided town of Mitrovica; 19 people are killed in the worst clashes between Serbs and ethnic Albanians since 1999.

October 2004. President Rugova's pro-independence Democratic League tops poll in general election, winning 47 seats in 120-seat parliament. Poll is boycotted by Serbs.

December 2004. Parliament reelects President Rugova and elects former rebel commander Ramush Haradinaj as prime minister. Mr. Haradinaj's party had entered into a coalition with the president's Democratic League.

February 2005. Serbian President Boris Tadic visits, promises to defend rights of Serbs in Kosovo.

March 2005. Mr. Haradinaj indicted to face UN war crimes tribunal in The Hague, Netherlands, and resigns as prime minister. He is succeeded by Bajram Kosumi. President Rugova unhurt when explosion rocks convoy of vehicles in which he is travelling through Pristina.

July 2005. Nearly-simultaneous blasts go off near UN, OSCE, and Kosovo parliament buildings in Pristina. No one is hurt.

August 2005. Two Serbs shot dead and two injured when their car is fired upon.

January 2006. President Rugova dies in Pristina after losing his battle with lung cancer. He is succeeded in February by Fatmir Sejdiu.

February 2006. UN-sponsored talks on the future status of Kosovo begin.

March 2006. Prime Minister Kosumi resigns following criticism of his performance from within his own party. He is succeeded by former KLA commander Agim Ceku.

July 2006. First direct talks since 1999 between ethnic Serbian and Kosovan leaders on future status of Kosovo take place in Vienna, Austria.

October 2006. Voters in a referendum in Serbia approve a new constitution which declares that Kosovo is an integral part of the country. Kosovo's Albanian majority boycotts the ballot, and UN sponsored talks on the future of the disputed province continue.

Independence Plan.

February 2007. UN envoy Martti Ahtisaari unveils a plan to set Kosovo on a path to independence, which is immediately welcomed by Kosovo Albanians and rejected by Serbia.

July 2007. U.S. and European Union (EU) redraft UN resolution to drop promise of independence at Russian insistence, replacing it with pledge to review situation if there is no breakthrough after proposed 4 months of talks with Serbia.

November 2007. Hasim Thaci emerges as winner in general elections.

February 2008. Kosovo declares independence. Serbia says declaration illegal. Europe's major powers and the United States recognize independence.

March 2008. Serb opponents of independence seize a UN courthouse in Mitrovica, and more than 100 people are injured in subsequent clashes with UN and NATO forces. A UN police officer is killed.

April 2008. Parliament adopts new constitution.

June 2008. New constitution transfers power to majority ethnic Albanian government after 9 years of UN transitional governance. Kosovo Serbs set up their own rival assembly in Mitrovica.

October 2008. The UN General Assembly votes to refer Kosovo's independence declaration to the International Court of Justice.

December 2008. EU mission (EULEX) takes over police, justice, and customs services from UN. Serbia accepts EU mission.

UNITED NATIONS INTERIM ADMINISTRATION MISSION IN KOSOVO (UNMIK) 1999 TO PRESENT

In June 1999, following a 78-day-long NATO campaign sanctioned by the UN Security Council, the UN was tasked to administer the region of Kosovo through a Chapter VII mandate of the UN Charter. The mission was established through its Interim Administration Mission in Kosovo (UNMIK), with the provision of a mandate to provide Kosovo with a "transitional administration while establishing and overseeing the development of provisional democratic self-governing institutions to ensure conditions for a peaceful and normal life for all inhabitants in Kosovo."[31]

In accordance with UN Security Council Resolution 1244, UNMIK established an international presence in Kosovo to strengthen the rule of law, among other things. Since 1999, UNMIK has assisted the state in developing Kosovo's Provisional Institutions of Self

Government (PISG). The state has increased its capacity to assume more administrative responsibilities. The *Standards for Kosovo*, established in 2002-03 are eight areas responding to Kosovo institutions that require reconstruction, or need to be constructed anew. The standards are meant to serve as benchmarks to help develop a fair, tolerant, and transparent Kosovo society, as well as improving the performance of particular public sectors, such as the reform of the police and judiciary within the context of the rule of law. After transition, Kosovo must build and maintain state and public institutions as accountable, professional, impartial bodies independent of political party patronage and control.[32] The eight areas of development are:

1. Functioning democratic institutions;
2. Rule of law;
3. Freedom of movement;
4. Sustainable returns and the rights of communities and their members;
5. Economy;
6. Property rights (including cultural heritage);
7. Pristina-Belgrade dialogue; and,
8. Kosovo Protection Corps (KPC).

For potential membership in the EU, the UN Development Programme describes Standards for Kosovo as:

> a Kosovo where public institutions are representative and democratic, where the rule of law is effective, respected, and accessible to all, where those internally displaced persons (IDPs) who wish to are free and able to return to Kosovo without hindrance, threat, or intimidation, where all individuals, regardless of ethnic background, can travel and work safely, and use their

languages (and where that use is respected) anywhere and in any institution of Kosovo, where the framework for a functioning market economy is in place and where the Kosovo Protection Corps operates strictly within its mandate; furthermore, the standards describe a Kosovo where Pristina is participating in successful dialogue with Belgrade and where Kosovo is in stable and peaceful relationships with its regional neighbours. In short, a truly multi-ethnic, stable and democratic Kosovo which is approaching European standards.[33]

The European Partnership Action Plan (EPAP) was developed to assist in Kosovo's European integration process and was adopted by the Kosovo government on August 9, 2006. This comprehensive document outlines measures that the Kosovo institutions intend to take to reach the priorities set out in the European Partnership and to fulfill the Standards for Kosovo. The EPAP not only responds to the priorities of the updated European Partnership, but it also aims to implement and accommodate the Standards for Kosovo process, thereby allowing for a joint approach to both processes.

Since 2008, UNMIK has transitioned its executive powers to most Kosovo institutions and adopted a monitoring and support mandate to further guide local institutions towards transparency, effectiveness, and anti-corruption. In December 2008, the EULEX took over the police, justice, and customs services from UNMIK. This was partially done to assist Kosovo with integrating into European society and systems.

It is important to note that Kosovo achieved independence from Serbia in 2008. Independence has affected Kosovo and Europe in many ways. In February 2008, the EU created a rule of law mission, which is the EU's biggest European security and defence policy (ESPD) operation.[34] The EU seeks to contribute to stabilization in the region of Kosovo and Serbia because they are of significant EU interest. Further conflict in this region would reduce the chances for EU membership for countries sharing the region.[35]

SECURITY SECTOR REFORM IN KOSOVO

Security sector reform (SSR) in Kosovo was undertaken by UNMIK based on its mandate outlined in UN Security Council Resolution 1244 of 1999. UNMIK was to perform "basic civilian administrative functions where and as long as required,"[36] which focused on the core institutions that would empower Kosovo to govern itself autonomously in the future. Much attention was devoted to reforming the police, the judiciary, and courts. These three institutions were to underwrite the rule of law in Kosovo and ensure a safe and democratic system of governance for the region (and eventually the country of Kosovo).

Resolution 1244 also mandated UNMIK to maintain "civil law and order, including establishing local police forces and meanwhile, through the deployment of international police personnel, to serve in Kosovo."[37]

To begin, the demilitarization of the KLA was completed by UNMIK. The demilitarization process offered "individual members of the KLA an opportunity to participate in a disciplined, professional, multiethnic civilian emergency corps."[38] The proposal to create a Kosovo Protection Corps (KPC) was an integral part of the demobilization, demilitarization and reintegration (DDR) process in Kosovo, which empowered the reform of the security sector.

From the beginning of the UNMIK mission, there were sufficient challenges to the development of an efficient, independent, and impartial criminal justice system with the competence to investigate and prosecute crimes. Such a justice system was vital if the rule of law was to become firmly rooted in Kosovo.[39] By 2002, only 3 years after the international intervention, "the capacity of Kosovo's judiciary, police service, and penal systems still needed to be strengthened, training for the civil service undertaken, accountability of Assembly members to their electorate enforced, and the rights of minorities protected."[40]

The majority of the UNMIK deployment was made up of international civilian police from countries such as Germany, Canada, France, United States, Russia, Pakistan, Malaysia, and the United Kingdom.[41] These peacekeepers were fundamental to the training, mentoring, and eventual monitoring of the Kosovo police, judiciary, and courts systems and assisted in the attainment of the standards for Kosovo, especially reestablishing a semblance of the rule of law for the people in the region. As the rule of law was strengthened, the lives improved for the people in the region. In addition, rule of law is a necessary foundation for a healthy flourishing market economy.

The OSCE, an European organization structured to deploy civilians to post-conflict environments and build local capacities to increase security and cooperation, has its own mandate in Kosovo and has worked with the UN mission to reestablish the rule of law. OSCE works very closely with their local field officers, which sets it apart from a typical UN mission. The OSCE usually has more locals employed than personnel that it deploys on a civilian mission.

One of the key challenges to the reconstruction of civil administration and institutions in Kosovo is the level of corruption within the existing social structures. Under the communist system, jobs were often filled by relatives and friends of people in higher-level positions. Nepotism in Kosovo remains a challenge that must be overcome. Misuse of public money and financial crime in government institutions has also remained a key challenge to meeting the standards for Kosovo, and engaging with the standards of Europe.

UNMIK viewed major reforms in the policing, judicial, and courts system as necessary to reduce corruption, nepotism, and other sub-standard activities that contributed to the deterioration of the rule of law. From the beginning, the emphasis of the mission has been on reforming the police.

Police.

The UNMIK Police has worked with the reformed Kosovo Police Service (KPS) to successfully investigate over 180,000 cases since 1999. They have worked to establish over 30 police stations and 13 border and boundary control points. UNMIK police and the KPS have policed Kosovo through a range of activities from patrols and traffic checks to investigations into serious crimes.[42] The KPS has learned the international policing standards for these activities from the civilian police deployed on UNMIK. The sharing of knowledge has matured the KPS's capacity to conduct policing in a timely standardized manner while contributing to the judiciary, courts, and corrections systems. Each of these systems requires equal strength and balance to uphold the rule of law and gain the trust of its citizens.

Up to 2007, in cooperation with OSCE, 8,270 KPS officers were recruited, trained, and deployed through the chain of command from the police stations up to the main headquarters level and into various specialized police departments. Between 2001 and 2008, the international intervention had between 3,300 police officers from more than 50 countries to approximately1,500 police officers from 31 countries. The policing program suggests that as more KPS officers are recruited, trained, and deployed, the number of internationally deployed OSCE and UNMIK police can be reduced so that eventually the KPS is administering its own institutions and the international intervention can end.

In addition to the individually deployed civilian police on the UNMIK and OSCE missions, approximately 499 Formed Police Units (FPU) from Pakistan, Romania, Poland, and the Ukraine were a part of the mission force. To further underwrite the rule of law, specialized agencies were developed to investigate the misuse of public money and financial crime (including money laundering) to further reduce corruption within Kosovo's public institutions.

The KPS has become a highly respected institution that enjoys the trust of its citizens. Because ethnicity was a driver of the Kosovo conflict, balanced ethnic representation was marked as a key component for the new KPS. The majority of the force is made up of ethnic Albanians, while Serbian and other minorities make up the rest. Like most police forces around the world, a gender balance has not been achieved in the KPS. The majority of serving police are men. The KPS holds the command of all police stations and most of the Regional Police Headquarters across Kosovo. UNMIK Police has assumed a supporting and monitoring role but retains overall supervisory authority of the UNMIK Police Commissioner. Further transition towards local capacities will continue until the mission is complete.

Department of Justice.

The UNMIK administered Department of Justice (DoJ) aims to function to European standards by prosecuting serious crime, including cases of corruption, terrorism, war crimes, and the riot cases from 2004. The new Provisional Criminal Code and Provisional Criminal Procedure Code of Kosovo came into effect in April 2004. UNMIK Regulation No. 2005/52 established the independent Kosovo Judicial Council and UNMIK Regulation No. 2005/53 established the Kosovo Ministry of Justice. As with the police sector, UNMIK has continued the transition of responsibilities of the DoJ to local institutions, the Ministry of Justice, and the Kosovo Judicial Council, and established the Kosovo Special Prosecutors Office to enable local prosecutors to take on more serious cases in the future, including corruption, organized crime, and crimes against public office. These cases will take more time to get into the justice system, as the challenge of corruption and illegal activities within public institutions remains, even within the justice and courts systems. To further strengthen the rule of law in Kosovo, the Judicial Inspection Unit (JIU) was established as an independent office mandated to investigate complaints of judicial and prosecutorial misconduct.

Courts.

The courts are responsible for the administration of justice in Kosovo in accordance with the applicable law. The court structure includes the Supreme Court of Kosovo, District Courts, Municipal Courts, and Courts of Minor Offences (including a High Court of Minor Offences). A Special Chamber of the Supreme Court deals with Kosovo Trust Agency related matters.

Organized crime poses a long-term threat to the stability of Kosovo's police, judiciary, and courts.

Linkages of political corruption with organized crime, coupled with weak rule of law, remain an obstacle in these institutions. Similar to many of the countries in the region, Kosovo is impacted by trafficking in human beings, drugs, and arms.[43]

Since UN Security Council Resolution 1244 in 1999, there have been no subsequent resolutions pertaining to Kosovo. This is unusual, as other case studies (for example, Liberia and Haiti) have had numerous resolutions addressing the changing nature of the mandate of a mission based on the context of peace and security in a mission area.[44]

KOSOVO RULE OF LAW

According to the report, *Implementing Security Sector Reform* co-published by the Center for Naval Analyses and Peacekeeping and Stability Operations Institute in 2008,[45] interventions — in particular stability operations — are pursued because the rule of law is not operating in a host nation. In the case of the host nation of Serbia, there was indeed a rule of law framework at work in Kosovo, however it was one that was unacceptable to the community of international states and actors. It is essential to consider that a region almost always has a rule of law framework that must be assessed through the SSR process. The assessment process must recognize and identify competing frameworks where they exist and determine the level of legitimacy that each enjoys among local communities.

Once the SSR assessment process has identified existing rule of law frameworks, SSR planning must determine which frameworks will be adopted and how they will be applied. Rule of law frameworks can be expected to change as powers are transitioned from the intervener to the host nation (or protectorate), and local capacities for the rule of law increase. SSR planning must both reflect and shape that change. Input from the host nation, or in the case of Kosovo, the autonomous civil administration of Kosovo, will be critical in both the rule of law assessment and in determining what frameworks to employ that would best suit Kosovo culture and society. When UNMIK and the OSCE arrived in Kosovo in 1999, the host nation government was not functional, yet means were identified to support host nation participation in the rule of law process because the mandate was to provide a "transitional administration while establishing and overseeing the development of provisional democratic self-governing institutions to ensure conditions for a peaceful and normal life for all inhabitants in Kosovo."[46]

Several critical issues can be addressed with respect to the rule of law by UNMIK and the Kosovo authorities. UNMIK and the Kosovo government had to determine to what extent the concept of shared sovereignty would apply and establish mechanisms and processes to implement shared sovereignty where required. In addition, UNMIK had to determine how Kosovo law would apply to reforms of the police, judiciary, courts, and corrections programs and implementers. It was important that UNMIK understand that the security sector reforms conducted under UN auspices would change over time and manifest differently when eventually led by the Kosovo institutions themselves, as UNMIK relinquished the lead and took on a monitoring role.

Decisions regarding the host nation rule of law framework will generate critical issues in related areas of governance beyond the reform of the security sector. The rule of law framework adopted by the international community for Kosovo will require changes to governance structures and processes, especially since Kosovo has gained its independence. The success of SSR is closely tied to the implementation of required changes in the political processes of governance. Because Kosovo is interested in being closely linked with Europe, this serves as an incentive to conform its other governance processes to such standards. Increased transparency, accountability, and effectiveness are hallmarks of change in Kosovo institutions.

The sequencing of the reform of police, judiciary, courts, and corrections is a critical component of SSR planning, especially for the judicial process. Questions regarding where to put the greatest efforts need to be assessed up front. International norms and standards and the sequencing and priorities of these standards are key questions in SSR. The sequencing and priorities that may work in one host nation do not work in another. In addition, some host nations are far from international norms and standards within their security sectors, so it becomes a matter of building the sector rather than reforming it. Kosovo, as a southeastern European entity, had modeled its security sectors based upon the standards and norms of the European community of states.

The rule of law framework adopted in Kosovo influences the relationship between central government authority and local governance structures, including customary and traditional structures. Issues related to nepotism, corruption, and other illegal acts are now challenged at the local level based on changes made to the centrally based institutions regarding rule of law.

The UNMIK-led reform of the Kosovo security sector determined a central role for the formal judicial process within the Kosovo criminal justice system.

As Kosovo already had a rule of law framework that included police, judiciary, courts, and corrections long before the outbreak of conflict with Serbian forces, there was a strong foundation upon which UNMIK and the OSCE built new capacities for strengthening the rule of law.

UNMIK planned the reform of the judicial process by determining staffing, systems, and new laws. There was little requirement for international judges to be invited into the program to lead the judicial process, rather there was a clear requirement to monitor judges and other staff within the context of strengthening the rule of law. The Kosovo judiciary system was relatively European by standard prior to the outbreak of conflict, therefore there were few traditional rule of law processes that did not in theory conform to the international standards of the interveners themselves. Despite having a rule of law framework that conformed in theory to international standards, it has taken much effort, time, and resources to create a fully functional rule of law process. It is important to note that it will take time for Kosovo to adopt a fully functional and legitimate host nation rule of law framework.

SUMMARY

Since the international community intervened in Kosovo, the region,

> has experienced a duality in governance, with the responsibilities shared between local and international authorities. This process of reserved competencies inhibits the clear division of responsibilities and creates confusion over lines of accountability. This situation is further aggravated by the lack of the culture of, and institutions for, coordination within the government.

Furthermore, governing institutions are viewed with considerable suspicion by the Serb community.[47]

The onus is on UNMIK, as well as on the international community and Kosovo's leaders, to fulfill their obligation to develop autonomous institutions for whatever final status awaits Kosovo. Democratic, effective, and ethnically representative government institutions must and can be built.[48]

Despite the UNMIK mission transitioning to the EULEX mission, there will remain a local capacity gap in filling the roles undertaken by the international police presence.[49] In addition, while international police forces are accepted by the Serb minority in Kosovo, the Kosovo police are not. This will remain an issue until a resolution of the ethnic divisions comes to pass in this region.

DISCUSSION QUESTIONS

1. Why was Kosovo a contested place within the Republic of Serbia in the 1980s and 1990s?

2. For what purpose or benefit for Kosovo were the NATO air-strikes against Milosevic's regime in Serbia?

3. What were the three areas of concern for the UN regarding the rule of law in Kosovo? Why are these three areas important when there is a lack of trust in government and widespread insecurity?

4. In what way did UNMIK build local capacities in the security sector to support the rule of law in Kosovo?

5. In your opinion, and compared against the tenets of accountability, transparency, and effectiveness, has UNMIK's SSR activities in Kosovo civil institutions been successful for the future of Kosovo as a democratic member of the European states?

ADDITIONAL REFERENCES

United Nations Resolutions relating to Kosovo.

United Nations Security Council Resolution 1199 (1998). *www.un.org/peace/kosovo/98sc1199.htm.*

United Nations Security Council Resolution 1203 (1998). *www.un.org/peace/kosovo/98sc1203.htm.*

United Nations Security Council Resolution 1244 (1999). *daccessdds.un.org/doc/UNDOC/GEN/N99/ 172/89/PDF/N9917289.pdf?OpenElement.*

Reports relating to Kosovo.

Dempsey, Thomas. ed. "Implementing Security Sector Reform" *Security Sector Reform Workshop, Interim Report* (Center for Naval Analyses and Peacekeeping and Stability Operations Institute, December 4, 2008). *https://pksoi.army.mil/Docs/Governance/SSR_ Workshop_Interim_Report.pdf.*

International Crisis Group. *Kosovo's Fragile Transition.* Europe Report N.196. September 25, 2008. *www. crisisgroup.org/home/index.cfm?id=5695&l=1.*

International Crisis Group. *A Kosovo Roadmap (II): Internal Benchmarks.* Europe Report N.125. 1

March 2002. *www.crisisgroup.org/home/index.cfm? id=1687&l=1.*

United Nations Security Council. *Report of the Secretary-General on the United Nations Interim Administration Mission in Kosovo.* S/1999/1250. December 23, 1999.

Weblinks.

UNMIK   *www.unmikonline.org/.*
OSCE- Kosovo   *www.osce.org/kosovo/.*
EU Pillar   *www.euinkosovo.org/.*
KFOR   *www.nato.int/KFOR/.*
Stability Pact   *www.stabilitypact.org/.*

LIBERIA:
NONSTATE SECURITY ACTORS

COUNTRY MAP

Source: Map of Liberia, No. 3775, Rev. 6, New York: United Nations Department of Public Information Cartographic Section, 2004.

LIBERIA BACKGROUNDER

Liberia's history is one of social and economic conflict. Some seeds of conflict were sown with the introduction of former slaves from the United States in the early 19th century, which caused social and class divisions between the Americo-Liberians and the indigenous population that continue to evolve over time. Through the brutality of colonial rule, dictatorship, and class division, the indigenous peoples were marginalized. The first uprising in

46

1822 by aboriginals against the colonists began over land ownership issues and ended in bloodshed and institutional ethnic hatred.

During the 20th century, the social divide between Americo-Liberians and the native population grew as the latter group continued to be excluded from the political and economic life of Liberia. Ethnically- and geographically-targeted violence took place at the hands of Liberia's first military. Liberia's modern military began as a colonial militia that was transformed into the Liberian Frontier Force. The force was made up of soldiers from the center and northwest of the country that were led by members of the Monravian elite. They committed violence against the Kru, Glebo, Bassa, and Krahn-speaking people in the southeast of the country, who were also largely excluded from recruitment.[50] The Frontier Force was encouraged to pay itself through looting, and it earned a reputation for brutality.[51] In 1962, the Frontier Force was renamed the Armed Forces of Liberia (AFL).

By the late 1970s, growing tensions between indigenous groups and the ruling Americo-Liberians reached a crisis point. In 1979 demonstrations and riots over the proposed increase in the price of rice prompted President William R. Tolbert to call in troops from neighboring Guinea to quell the rebellion. Tolbert was executed in 1980 after a band of soldiers under the leadership of Master Sergeant Samuel Doe staged a *coup d'état* and declared a military *junta*. The brutal leadership of the People's Redemption Council headed by Doe consolidated power by violently silencing critics through wide-scale strategic corruption. Being a noncommissioned officer (NCO), Doe promoted fellow NCOs and further militarized the government by giving military rank and title to civilian ministers.

In 1985, after a promised return to democratic rule, Doe led the National Democratic Party of Liberia (NDPL) to victory after an election that was considered to be fraudulent. During this period, Thomas Quiwonkpa, a former ally of Doe and an ethnic Dan, led an unsuccessful coup resulting in reprisals against Mano and Dan populations by Doe's Krahn-majority army. The grievances from these attacks assisted Charles Taylor, a former aide to the Doe regime, with the recruitment of approximately 5,000 young fighters.

Tensions boiled over in 1989 when Charles Taylor led members of the National Patriotic Front of Liberia (NPFL) into clashes with the AFL loyal to the President. Taylor, an Americo-Liberian, was educated in the United States and trained in insurgency tactics in Libya.[52] The NPFL was backed by regular troops from neighboring states, and was responsible for gross human rights abuses and murder targeting the Krahn and Mandingo groups loyal to Doe. To further add to the complex dynamics of the conflict, the Gio ethnic community, who are mainly Muslim, rallied around Prince Johnson who broke from the NPFL. Johnson captured and brutally murdered Doe on national television in September 1990.

HISTORY OF INTERNATIONAL ENGAGEMENT

Efforts to end the conflict began in 1990 when the Economic Community of West African States (ECOWAS) established a military observer group (ECOMOG). ECOMOG was comprised of 4,000 troops from 15 African states and was initially supported by both the NDPL and troops loyal to Johnson. Taylor's

NPFL rejected ECOMOG's legitimacy, claiming it was allied with AFL troops. In 1991 the NPFL agreed to disarm and set up an Interim Government of National Unity, but in 1992 it attacked ECOWAS peacekeepers in Monrovia. The peacekeepers responded by bombing NPFL positions, pushing it back outside the capital and into the countryside.

The United Nations (UN) backed ECOWAS's attempts to find a diplomatic and humanitarian solution to the Liberian civil war. In December 1990, assistance was provided by front line UN support agencies and coordinated by the UN Special Coordinator's Office in Liberia (UNSCOL), based in the capital, Monrovia. There was no direct Security Council involvement in the civil war until December 1992, when Resolution 788 (1992) was adopted, calling for an arms embargo on Liberia.[53] In July 1993, the warring factions met with diplomatic representatives of ECOWAS, the UN, and the Organization of African Unity in Cotonou, Benin, and agreed on a ceasefire effective on August 1, 1993, as well as the establishment of a National Transitional Government.[54] In 1994, warring parties agreed on a disarmament timetable.

The Security Council adopted Resolution 866 (1993) to establish the United Nations Observer Mission in Liberia (UNOMIL), which augmented ECOMOG in implementing the Cotonou Agreement. UNOMIL's initial mandate included both a military and civilian component. Military forces were tasked to monitor the ceasefire agreement and weapons embargo, as well as begin the process of disarming and demobilizing former combatants. The civilian and humanitarian mandate required UN agencies to coordinate with the newly formed transitional government, comprised of the three warring parties, to prepare for general elections.

Despite the optimism surrounding Cotonou, an uneasy balance within the transitional government failed along ethnic lines. As the political rift intensified, fighting erupted in various regions, putting the disarmament and demobilization program in peril. By October 1994, the country slipped backed into a state of civil war as the warring factions split further. The subsequent crisis resulted in a deteriorating humanitarian situation as factional fighting cut off agencies from displaced populations in need of aid and assistance. On October 21, 1994, the Security Council adopted Resolution 950 (1994) to extend UNOMIL's mission at the request of ECOWAS.[55]

The diplomatic and military situation throughout 1995 remained tenuous as factions continued the fighting, which added to the humanitarian crisis throughout Liberia. The UN continued to extend the operational mandate of UNOMIL through Resolutions 972, 985, and 1001 (1995). However, the warring parties failed to adhere to their own commitments with little incentive to engage in the peace process.

The threat to withdraw UNOMIL after the end of its fourth extension by the Security Council resulted in pressure for ECOWAS to strengthen its efforts to seek a comprehensive ceasefire during July and August. Agreement was finally reached on August 19, 1995, in Abuja, Nigeria. The agreement called for a formal ceasefire to begin on August 26, the creation of a Ruling Council, and the setting of an election date for August 20, 1996. For the rest of the year and into 1996, violations of the ceasefire agreement threatened to plunge Liberia back into civil war. By April 1996, fighting spread into Monrovia. On May 26, 1996, ECOWAS was able to broker a ceasefire and put the political process back on track as outlined in the Abuja Agreement.

The mandate of UNOMIL was further extended as the process of preparing Liberia for a return to democracy continued throughout the later half of 1996. The ceasefire held despite continued political maneuvering and an assassination attempt on Charles Taylor. During the course of the conflict, 150,000 people were killed while another 800,000 Liberians had fled to other countries in the region.[56] In August 1996, ECOWAS peacekeepers initiated a program to disarm, clear land mines, reopen roads, and otherwise facilitate the return of refugees and internally displaced persons. With the increased incentive of a food ration from the World Food Program, former combatants gladly turned over their firearms, and the disarmament and demobilization program was completed in February 1997. On July 24, 1997, after an election that was declared free and fair by international observers, Charles Taylor was elected president, and his National Patriotic Party (NPP) won a majority in the National Assembly. With a new government in place, UNOMIL was ended, and an UN peace-building support office (UNOL) was established to assist in the reconciliation and development process.

Despite increased stability within Liberia, tensions rose between it and its neighbors. In January 1999, Ghana and Nigeria accused Liberia of supporting Revolutionary United Front (RUF) rebels in Sierra Leone. As a result, the United States and Britain threatened to suspend aid to Liberia. Fighting erupted along the Guinean border as forces on each side engaged in attacks and counterattacks. Taylor's government announced in February 2001 that Sierra Leonean rebel leader Sam Bockarie had left the country, by May the UN Security Council reinstated its arms embargo as punishment for Taylor's *weapons for diamonds* trade with Sierra Leonean rebels. It also introduced an export embargo on Liberian diamonds to curb the flow of *blood diamonds*, which helped to fund the Liberian conflict as well as subregional armed conflicts. Similarly, logging was banned due to concerns over its role in funding criminal activity.

Despite ongoing efforts by UNOL, renewed fighting began as rifts widened between government and opposition groups. By February 2002, Taylor's government declared a state of emergency, and by March 2003 rebels had advanced within 10 km of the capital. On July 8, 2003, Taylor accepted an offer of asylum from Nigeria after growing pressure due to war crime accusations over alleged support to rebel factions in Sierra Leone and his role in diamond trafficking.

On August 1, 2003, the Security Council adopted Resolution 1497 to establish a multinational stabilization force.[57] Taylor fled the country after handing over power to his deputy, Moses Blah. U.S. troops arrived in Liberia. The Interim government and warring factions gathered in Accra to establish a ceasefire brokered by ECOWAS. The Accra Comprehensive Peace Agreement (CPA) was signed in August 2003, essentially bringing an end to 14 years of conflict. Gyude Bryant was chosen to head the new administration. During the course of the conflict, 250,000 people were killed, while another one million were displaced, out of a population of approximately three million people.

On September 19, 2003, the Security Council adopted Resolution 1509 (2003) establishing the United Nations Mission in Liberia (UNMIL). The new mandate of the peacekeeping mission was to support the peace process, provide continued assistance to humanitarian and human rights operations, support security sector reform, and provide protection to UN personnel.

On October 1, 2003, UNMIL took over peacekeeping operations from ECOWAS, and the West African troops were *rehatted* as UN blue helmets.[58] U.S. troops left the country, and thousands of UN troops were deployed. On November 11, 2005, the UNSC Resolution 1538 (2005) increased the mandate to include the capture and transfer of Charles Taylor to face trial. While he had been given political asylum in Nigeria, he was arrested on war crimes charges in June 2006. He is currently on trial in The Hague for war crimes and crimes against humanity.

CONTEMPORARY CONTEXT

Progress.

On November 23, 2005, Ellen Sirleaf-Johnson became the first female president on the African continent when she was elected president of Liberia, quite a historic event. This achievement offers hope for a country with a history of deep ethnic and social divisions and gender inequities. President Sirleaf-Johnson has implemented strong economic and political reforms, including policies aimed at reducing corruption, winning the support of international donors, and promoting private investment.

Progress towards sustainable peace and security is evident as real gross domestic product (GDP) growth is strong, development has accelerated, army reform and disarmament, demobilization and reintegration (DDR) have progressed, voluntary repatriation of refugees is high, and the Truth and Reconciliation Commission (TRC) has been launched. UN records indicate that between 2003 and 2004 more than 100,000 former combatants[59] were demobilized and received a transitional payment. In June 2006, the UN Security Council lightened its arms embargo to permit Liberia to arm its newly trained security forces. By April 2007, the embargo on Liberian diamond exports was lifted. The government undertook a review of all mining contracts and concessions in late 2006 and is now participating in the *Kimberley Process*, an international process that aims to reduce the sale of blood diamonds. In March 2008, Liberia conducted its first census since 1984. The government finalized a National Security Strategy paper in late 2008 which, upon official release, is hoped to give much-needed clarity to the roles and responsibilities of the security forces.

Challenges.

Despite progress, challenges to security and governance remain. While GDP growth has been strong, much of it is accounted for by reconstruction efforts, while Liberia remains dependent on the support of international donors. More than 80 percent of Liberia's population is illiterate and live below the poverty line, while almost an entire generation did not receive any formal primary education because of the constraints caused by violent armed conflict and political corruption. An estimated 80 percent of Liberians are unemployed, but exact numbers are difficult to determine due to the extensive informal sector.[60] The growing youth population places further constraints on the developing economy, while public sector employment has fallen due to government reforms and restructuring.

The legacies of conflict continue to plague the country. Despite reportedly high disarmament and demobilization levels, the validity of these numbers have since been put into question and the reintegration process has not met with comparable success.[61] Due to increased gun violence, in December 2008 the UN Security Council once again extended its arms and travel embargoes for another year. The UN Envoy to Liberia, Ms. Ellen Margrethe Loj, has appealed to Liberian chiefs, elders, and community leaders to take a stand to stop violence against women.[62] Rape was used as a tool of warfare during the armed conflict and remains the most common serious crime in Liberia today. Public complaints about police corruption, including extortion, are also reminiscent of the conflict era. In addition, municipal elections have not been held since May 1985 due to instability and insufficient finances.

Further reforms are needed in all of the security sectors, and the fragile security situation requires the continued presence of UNMIL. The UN Security Council extended the mandate of UNMIL until September 30, 2009, with the passing of Resolution 1836 (2008). The population's expectations for concrete peace dividends are high, while the rebuilding process will take many years.

Overview.

The UN Secretary-General emphasized to the Security Council the importance of security sector reform (SSR) in Liberia, declaring that: "Our common strategic goal is to ensure that Liberia has a solid security sector—one that can stand on its own feet before UNMIL completes its withdrawal."[63] With the reduction in military personnel by 1,460, UNMIL's focus shifted to stabilizing the rule of law in Liberia. Accordingly, the Security Council approved the augmentation of UNMIL police officers by 240, for a total of 845 personnel in two formed police units "to provide strategic advice and expertise in specialized fields, provide operational support to regular policing activities, and react to urgent security incidents."[64] However, support will need to be sustained over time, as one presidential advisor stated, "we are about 40 percent of the way there with the police and 55 percent with the army."[65] Thus, much remains to be done in order to achieve successful and sustainable security sector reform in Liberia.

SECURITY SECTOR REFORM IN LIBERIA

The *Security Sector Reform Workshop, Interim Report* co-published by the Center for Naval Analyses and the Peacekeeping and Stability Operations Institute (2008)[66] points to nonstate actors as important stakeholders in the SSR process. Potentially, nonstate security actors can contribute to the provision of security at the community level. They can also act as force multipliers to the intervening forces if they are persuaded to be collaborative partners. On the other hand, nonstate security actors can act as spoilers if they are not brought into the reform process and instead feel isolated from it.

Nonstate security actors have an integral role to play in Liberia's SSR process, the success of which may be contingent on the effective management and inclusion of these important stakeholders. In particular, ex-combatants, unemployed youth, and women need to be permitted to contribute to local ownership of the SSR process. Various factors increase the risk that vulnerable groups could instead have a destabilizing influence on the SSR process. These risk factors include the global economic and food crisis compounded by the volatility of an emerging economy with pervasive poverty and high unemployment rates, the spread of HIV/AIDS, subregional insecurity, small arms availability, as well as the prevalence of land disputes, criminal influences, and grievances deriving from ineffective rule of law and resulting in extra-judicial measures and mob violence.

The next section includes an overview of each of these nonstate actors and an assessment of their current or potential imprint on the Liberian security sector landscape. It is followed by an overview of the community-based actors and mechanisms that have been filling the security gap as the state-centered reform of the security sector has been underway.

NONSTATE ACTORS CHALLENGING SSR IN LIBERIA

The security situation in Liberia remains tenuous for a number of reasons that contribute to the heightened risk of nonstate actors becoming spoilers. One of the primary reasons is due to economic constraints and high unemployment. An unemployment rate at 80 percent does not help encourage young men to make a living without a gun, nor does it facilitate the reintegration of former combatants into sustainable livelihoods within a normalized society. Both groups are vulnerable to recruitment into domestic and foreign militia that undermine the authority of, and work in opposition to, the Liberian government. History has also shown a high recruitment of women combatants in Liberia, they accounted for 30 to 40 percent of former combatants.[67] It is also important to include Liberian women in this discussion, due to their vulnerability to becoming potential combatants, as well as the disproportionate impact that conflict has on women in general.

Ex-Combatants.

Historically, militia groups played a role in the Liberian conflict, and they also have potential to impact the ongoing security situation. Rebel militia, such as the Liberians United for Reconciliation and Democracy (LURD) and the Movement for Democracy in Liberia (MODEL), successfully fought to oust Taylor in 2003. Illegitimate Liberian administrations had to use militia to acquire and consolidate power, as well as to protect and control the exploitation of the country's natural resources. As power shifted, members of these forces disintegrated into warring militias. Widespread human rights abuses were committed by militia on both sides of the conflict, and the use of rape, pillaging, and looting as weapons of warfare were common practices.

Militia groups continue to pose a threat to stability in Liberia. According to the 2007 RAND report that was commissioned by the U.S. and Liberian governments, the continued existence of rebel group command structures remain a security concern.[68] A study by the International Crisis Group argued that disarmament numbers are questionable since the DDR process did not require registrants to prove their claims and did not question alleged combatants that did not have any weapons to turn in.[69] It was reported that former rebel commanders had provided the required ammunition to their business contacts so they could receive the disarmament payments.

Even if disarmament and demobilization has been somewhat successful, the reintegration process has not been. The challenges of reintegrating former combatants have been compounded by the fact that the new army did not draw from the pool of ex-combatants and instead chose fresh recruits. Regardless of justifications for this decision, it has nonetheless contributed to high levels of unemployment and frustration. In addition, grievances about outstanding disarmament and pension payments have at times erupted into violence.[70] In fact, some have argued that the very act of making disarmament and demobilization payments has helped to reinforce the conditioning that violence, or the threat thereof, is rewarded and viewed as a vital means to achieve whatever the desired end.[71] These patterns of corruption continue to undermine the reform of the security sector in Liberia because combatants were not truly disarmed, demobilized, or reintegrated into society, thereby remaining a threat to the rule of law and to the international community of donors attempting to build local security sector capacities.

Youth.

Even as ex-combatants get older and pose less of a risk, a large population of unemployed youth are developing their own grievances against the political and economic systems of Liberia. If excluded and isolated from the process, unemployed youth represent a threat to effective and sustainable SSR. Historically, Liberian youth have been marginalized and exploited.[72] This is a legacy that will need to be overcome. Estimates place unemployment rates at around 80 percent,[73] while Liberian youth (15-35 years)[74] make up 55-60 percent of the country's population. Young people account for the vast majority of the population that was affected by the conflict, as many of them were internally displaced and became refugees or combatants.[75] Though precise numbers are difficult to determine, it is likely that unemployed youth affected by conflict make up a significant portion of Liberia's population.

Due to their potential to have either a significant stabilizing or destabilizing influence depending on how they are managed, it is paramount that Liberian youth are adequately considered in, as well as empowered to contribute to, the national SSR process. In its Development Assistance Framework for Liberia, the United Nations Development Programme (UNDP) argued that the inclusion and empowerment of youth in the economy, politics, as well as conflict prevention and management are essential to reducing overall poverty and promoting stability.[76] If ignored, youth unemployment, coupled with the availability of small arms and pervasive poverty, could further undermine the rule of law and be a counter-force to the reforms of the security sector developed by the international community and the host nation of Liberia. Not only is sustainable peace in Liberia threatened because of youth issues, there is the risk of this threat impacting the entire region.

Women.

Women have been particularly affected by armed conflict in Liberia, because many now lack basic education and livelihood skills. During the conflict, more than 25,000 Liberian women chose to take up arms for various reasons, including self-protection from sexual violence, desire to avenge the death of family members, peer pressure, material gain, and survival.[77] These women accounted for 30 to 40 percent of armed combatants. When they initially returned following the conflict, many were met with hostility and some continue to face social stigmatization and isolation from their families and communities. In addition, women remain targets of sexual violence, which has long-term effects not only on their own well-being, but also on the communities in which they live.

Women have played a positive role in post-conflict stabilization and reconstruction in other post-conflict countries and have the potential to do the same in Liberia. However, more work needs to be done to empower women in the reform of the security sector. Reform efforts in support of women have met with some success, such as the graduation of Liberia's first all-female class of police officers from the Liberia Police Academy in early 2008. The representation of women in the Liberian National Police (LNP) has increased, yet less than 10 percent of LNP are women. Nevertheless, it is recognized that Liberia is moving in the right direction in this area, as Liberia's President Sirleaf-Johnson is committed to reforming the security sector in a way that supports the protection and empowerment of women. This is evident through the introduction of gender units within the police, as well as the development of a legal framework that includes laws that help protect against sexual and gender-based violence.[78] Most recently, in its Poverty Reduction Strategy, the Liberian government outlined its goal of achieving 20 percent female participation in the military and other security agencies, and it also placed gender justice and equality as core values in its reform of governance and the rule of law.

Aside from unemployed and alienated female ex-combatants, women do not pose a threat to the SSR process in the same way as unemployed youth do. Nevertheless, an inclusive and locally owned SSR will need to continue to support the reintegration of female ex-combatants and capacity development of women in general, in addition to strengthening training for male security forces to help them effectively address the high occurrence of sexual and gender-based violence in Liberia.[79]

COMMUNITY-BASED SECURITY ACTORS AND MECHANISMS

Communities have developed local approaches to provide for their own security and justice in the absence of state-based capacity to provide appropriate mechanisms in support of security and the rule of law. These community-based approaches include official and unofficial local patrols, vigilantes, work-based associations, and police, among others. This section discusses these approaches, beginning with the conditions that have inspired them. It includes some of the issues raised by these approaches and their implications on Liberia's process for SSR.

State Police: Capacity and Reach.

Liberia's conflict left the state police decimated. Through the vetting process, 60 percent of the state police force was disbanded following the end of the armed conflict.[80] For the past 5 years, the United Nations Mission in Liberia (UNMIL) has been actively engaged in helping to boost police numbers and capacity with the recruitment, vetting, and training of the LNP. It has also assisted its international partners with building police stations and barracks, and providing vehicles and other logistical equipment.[81] The target of commissioning 3,500 LNP officers was reached in early 2008, including 1,000 officers who had received specialized training.[82] Female representation in the police force has increased, with the support of the first deployed all-women formed police unit from India, among other measures.[83] However, according to a March 2008 study on SSR in Liberia, overall training outcomes for the LNP have been poor.[84]

In a population of three million people, 3,500 police are insufficient to uphold laws, provide security, perform duties such as investigations, and mediate grievances through community policing initiatives. With personnel confined mostly to urban centers and main roads, the LNP still does not have the capacity to serve all of the country. Despite international assistance, the LNP struggle with an escalation in crime, including robberies, theft, and assaults, that is becoming endemic. In 2008, the crime rate surpassed levels from every year since 2004.[85] To address the police capacity gaps, the target number of trained police has been raised to 6,000.[86]

Rural areas in particular represent security vacuums that are not currently being filled by the state police architecture. People in remote areas complain that police, when they do come to their areas, do not leave the main roads to conduct patrols. When police are called to a crime or accident, they sometimes take a whole day to respond, if they answer the phone at all.[87] The UN has urged the LNP to provide protection to all Liberians, rather than a select few.[88]

While rural communities are the most disadvantaged by the lack of police capacity and reach, the problem is also prevalent in the Liberian capital, Monrovia. With the destruction caused by the armed conflict, there has been a flood of people into urban centers, particularly Monrovia. UN estimates suggest approximately 59 percent of the population live in urban centers.[89] Despite the centralization of the police in urban centers, such as Monrovia, there has been an escalation of violent crime in the capital and the police have been ineffective in combating it.[90]

State Police: Internal Discipline. Despite the vetting process and training, human rights abuses still plague the current LNP. Some state police from the armed conflict-era have maintained their positions but have yet to be professionalized and held accountable, so a culture of impunity prevails in the forces. Due to continued government delays in making the Independent National Commission on Human Rights operational, the human rights situation remains problematic and undermines the rule of law in Liberia.[91]

Accusations of police brutality and corruption are compromising public confidence. Typically, in the past the police were not paid wages and were instead expected to extort bribes from civilians.[92] This legacy continues. In an address to the LNP, the UN Envoy stressed the need for them to be professional, respect human rights, and otherwise act in accordance with the police code of ethics. A 2008 study that discussed the poor training outcomes for the LNP pointed to low morale and discipline coupled with extremely poor leadership and management as being at the root of the problem.[93] In addition, these problems worsen because there is no coherent national security strategy, let alone a national crime prevention strategy.[94] While the government finalized a National Security Strategy paper in late 2008, it has yet to be officially launched. Without these issues being fully addressed, police brutality and extortion may remain as legacies of the armed conflict period.

Community-based Approaches to Policing. During the conflict, Liberia's security forces were a mixture of the armed forces, LURD, and the MODEL rebel units, militias, and paramilitary groups.[95] For 2 years after the conflict ended, military and rebel factions continued to coerce the public while they were awarded senior government positions without earning them through merit.[96] As a result, communities were not eager to work with the state on police reform.[97] Similarly, the state was not intent on including local communities in the reform process.[98]

The UN Police (UNPOL) section of UNMIL took over training and the development of policing policy; however, in an effort to expedite the process, they reintroduced approaches used in Bosnia-Herzegovina and elsewhere that did not particularly work well in the Liberian context.[99] The Sirleaf-Johnson administration has adopted UNMIL's state-centered approach to policing, which is not consistent with existing community-based approaches and mechanisms.[100]

For the first few years following the armed conflict, the streets of Monrovia were patrolled at night by vigilante groups and task forces of male youth.[101] Initially they found support from the Minister of Justice at the time, who encouraged communities to defend themselves through such groups.[102] Following cases of suspected robbers being beaten to death, human rights groups protested this decision, and the groups were ordered to disband.

However, the community-based groups were provided the option of joining the official Community Police Forums, which in theory provide an official link between the rural communities and the state police. Although in practice they receive very little state support and funding, and citizens are not provided with many opportunities for true participation.[103] Moreover, the LNP prefer to see the role of community-based police as serving to complement their own activities rather than acting in partnership;[104] this is evidenced by the unidirectional flow of information between them. Thus, community-based police in Liberia are not autonomous from the state police, but their connection is tenuous.

The community-based vigilante groups and task forces do not appear to have actually disbanded.[105] Some groups that chose to participate in the Community Police Forum lost support due to threats from criminals and a lack of motivation.[106] As a result of these factors and official disapproval, local patrols are not as visible as they were following the armed conflict. There are, nevertheless, reports of unofficial community-based mechanisms and activities. Due to the lack of confidence in the police's ability to manage the increase in armed robbery in the capital, locals in Monrovia have reportedly organized civilian night patrol teams since they feel that: "We have no choice but to provide security for ourselves."[107] There are also reports from elsewhere in the country, where local groups have formed to control the entry points into their communities at night.[108] However, when these groups do apprehend suspected criminals, they turn them over to the state police, but not always without beating them first.

There are numerous forms of community-based security and justice mechanisms in Liberia. Work-based associations and police are particularly prominent.[109] Rather than going to state authorities with information, these groups typically try to investigate and resolve disputes themselves. While aiming for reconciliation, they punish members for bad conduct with fines, and as a last resort they expel members.[110] Other mechanisms include customary chiefs, market vendors' committees, taxi drivers' associations, justice nongovernmental organizations (NGOs), and town courts.[111] The latter is governed by customary law and led by chiefs, governors, and other local officials,[112] while punishment is delivered through fines.[113] Dispute resolution through mediation, however, is preferred to punishment.[114]

Through their community-based approaches and mechanisms, Liberians are managing without the strong presence of the state police. Nevertheless, their preference would be to see more of the state police, but instead they are left with a sense of abandonment.[115] Continued frustration over lack of police responsiveness frequently emerges through extra-judicial measures being taken and escalates into mob violence. Despite the preference for conflict resolution at the local level, "corporal punishment is not far out of everyone's minds and, of course, is the normal practice of mob justice."[116] In reaction to a case of mob violence resulting in murder, the UN Envoy to Liberia, Ms. Ellen Margrethe Loj, appealed to Liberians to take a stand against all forms of violence.[117] She also called on leaders in the local community to help stop violence against women. Even as she promoted community-based approaches to these issues, she advised that state-based "wheels of justice turn slowly," and that people should "let the police and the courts do their work."[118] The leaders responded by apologizing and promising that the local community would "bring the leaders of the mob to justice"[119] — therefore suggesting that community-based justice would persist.

SUMMARY

While Liberia may have turned a page in its history with the end of the 14-year armed conflict, efforts need to be sustained to ensure that the root causes of conflict do not reemerge to undermine the fragile progress that has been made. Where security gaps remain and frustration endures, local communities will continue to resort to extra-judicial measures, including gun violence and mob justice. Liberians, particularly youth, ex-combatants, and women, need to be provided with the peace dividends and the capacity to help ensure that progress is solidified and SSR is sustainable, accountable, transparent, and effective.

Attempts to link communities to the official state security infrastructure through the Community Police Forum have largely failed. A decentralized and ad hoc system for providing security has instead emerged and threatens to undermine the authority and legitimacy of the current administration under President Sirleaf-Johnson. Much stronger efforts need to be made for the government in Liberia to extend its reach and enhance its legitimacy in the eyes of its population by securing a monopoly on the use of force and being the principal provider of security for the Liberian people.

SSR in Liberia needs to be state-driven, locally-owned, and inclusive. While community-based measures and approaches may continue to be applied to reinforce the state security system and architecture, they should not be applied in isolation from it. Unemployed youth, women, and ex-combatants have the potential to make a positive contribution to stability in Liberia; that is, if their existing potential is effectively harnessed. To be truly sustainable, accountable, transparent, and effective, locally owned and state-driven SSR processes need to incorporate, rather than isolate, these important nonstate actors and community-based approaches.

DISCUSSION QUESTIONS

1. What types of tension were introduced to Liberia with the repatriation of the Americo-Liberian slave population?

2. Why did ECOWAS attempt to intervene in Liberia in the 1990s? What African interests were they attempting to protect?

3. What was the process of reforming the security sector in Liberia after the UN established a peace agreement between warring factions?

4. In what way did the UN interventions build local capacities in the security sector to support the rule of law in Liberia? How have nonstate actors impacted this process?

5. In your opinion, and compared against the tenets of accountability, transparency and effectiveness, have UN SSR activities in Liberia related to police reforms been successful in establishing sustainable peace and security?

ADDITIONAL REFERENCES

United Nations Resolutions Relating to Liberia.

United Nations Security Council Resolution 788 (1992). *daccessdds.un.org/doc/UNDOC/GEN/N93/010/46/IMG/N9301046.pdf?OpenElement.*

United Nations Security Council Resolution 866 (1993). *daccessdds.un.org/doc/UNDOC/GEN/N93/513/89/PDF/N9351389.pdf?OpenElement.*

United Nations Security Council Resolution 1497 (2003). *daccessdds.un.org/doc/UNDOC/GEN/N03/449/48/PDF/N0344948.pdf?OpenElement.*

United Nations Security Council Resolution 1836 (2008). *www.reliefweb.intrw/rwb.nsf/db900sid/VDUX-7JXQS2?OpenDocument&rc=1&cc=lbr.*

United Nations Security Council Resolution 9547 (2008). *www.un.org/News/Press/docs/2008/sc9547.doc.htm.*

Reports Relating to Liberia.

Aboagye, Festus, and Martin Rupiya. "Enhancing Post-Conflict Democratic Governance Through Effective Security Sector Reform in Liberia," Executive Summary, 2005. *www.issafrica.org/pubs/Books/TortuousRoad/Chap11.pdf.*

Baker, Bruce. "Post-war Policing by Communities in Sierra Leone, Liberia, Rwanda," in *Democracy and Security, Vol. 3, No. 2* 2007, pp. 215-236. *www.ssrnetwork.net/upload_files/3690.pdf.*

Crane, Keith, David Gompert, Olga Oliker, K. Jack Riley, and Brooke Stearns. "Making Liberia Safe: Transformation of the National Security Sector," Monograph, RAND, 2007. *www.rand.org/pubs/monographs/2007/RAND_MG529.pdf .*

Economist Intelligence Unit. "Country Report: Liberia," March 2009. *www.eiu.com/report_dl.asp?issue_id=1843610169&mode=pdf&rf=0.*

International Crisis Group. "Liberia: Uneven Progress in Security Sector Reform." *Africa Report N°148,* Jan. 13, 2009. *www.crisisgroup.org/home/index.cfm?id =5867&l=1.*

Malan, Mark. "Security Sector Reform in Liberia: Mixed Results from Humble Beginnings," Carlisle, PA: Strategic Studies Institute, U.S. Army War College, 2008. *www.strategicstudiesinstitute.army.mil/pdffiles/ pub855.pdf.*

United Nations Security Council. "Eighteenth progress report of the Secretary-General on the United Nations Mission in Liberia (S/2009/86)," Feb. 10, 2009. *www.reliefweb.int/rw/rwb.nsf/retrieveattachme nts?openagent&shortid=EGUA-7P8TD6&file=Full_ Report.pdf.*

Weblinks.

Central Intelligence Agency. "The World Factbook: Liberia." *https://www.cia.gov/library/publications/the- world-factbook/geos/li.html#Govt.*

GFN-SSR Library. *www.ssrnetwork.net/document_library /index.php.*

Institute for Security Studies (ISS). "SSR" - *www.iss. co.za/index.php?link_id=31&link_type=12&tmpl_ id=2.*

"Country File: Liberia" - *www.issafrica.org/index.php? link_id=14&slink_id=3930&link type=12&slink_type= 12&tmpl_id=3&link_country_id=45.*

International Crisis Group (ICG). *www.crisisgroup.org*.

OECD DAC. *www.oecd.org/department/0,2688,en_2649_33721_1_1_1_1_1,00.html*.

UN DPKO Mission Page. *www.un.org/Depts/dpko/missions/unmil/*.

UNMIL Mission Page. *www.unmil.org/*.

UN OCHA – Relief Web. *www.reliefweb.int/rw/dbc.nsf/doc104?OpenForm&rc=1&cc=lbr*.

UN DPKO – SSR Team, Office of Rule of Law and Security Institutions. *www.un.org/Depts/dpko/dpko/orolsi.shtml*.

HAITI:
POLICE AND LAW ENFORCEMENT

COUNTRY MAP

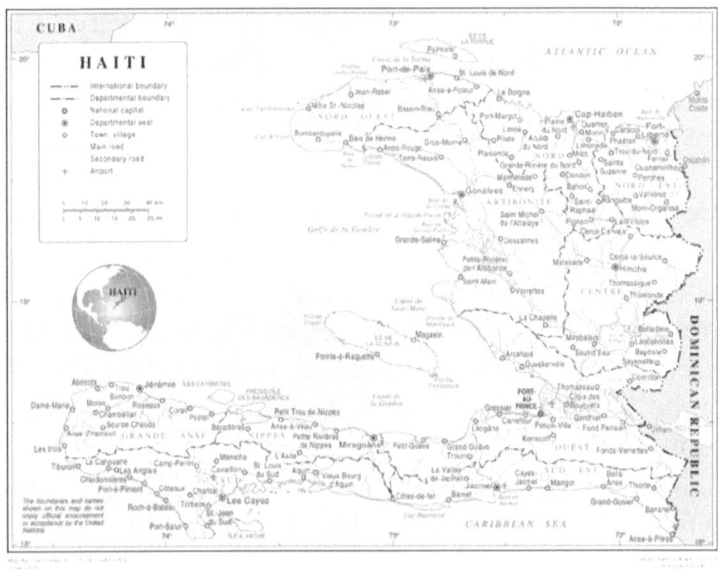

Source: Map of Haiti, No. 3855, Rev. 4, New York: United Nations Cartographic Section, 2008.

HAITI BACKGROUNDER

Located in the Caribbean, Haiti occupies the western one-third of the island of Hispaniola, which it shares with the Dominican Republic. The island spans 27,750 kilometres and is located between the Caribbean Sea and the North Atlantic Ocean. Just over 8 million people live in Haiti. It is a densely populated island, particularly in urban areas such as Port-au-Prince. On average, 293 people occupy each square kilometer in Haiti. About 95 percent of the population is of African descent. The other 5 percent are of mixed Caucasian-African ancestry, while a few people in Haiti have European or Levantine heritage. The state religion is Roman Catholicism. Haiti's second major religion is Protestant (16 percent), and approximately half of Haitians practice Voodoo. The majority of the population is female. Haiti's population is young, with a median age of 18 years. The two official languages are French and Haitian Creole.

At its inception, Haiti was a country with a promising future. As the world's first black republic, Haiti experienced the only successful slave revolution in history when it liberated itself from Napoleon's forces at the Battle of Vertières on November 18, 1803. Haiti then became the second independent country in the New World when it declared its independence from France on January 1, 1804.

Despite the hope that its newfound independence generated, its leadership, like many countries in the Americas, has been historically dominated by dictators. During its formative years, Haiti experienced a series of dictatorships, under Jean-Jacques Dessalines (1804-06), Alexandre Pétion and Henri Christophe (1806-20), and Jean-Pierre Boyer (1820-43). In the international realm, France was reluctant to recognize Haiti's independence, and demanded that Haiti compensate the French planters for their losses during the revolution. Haiti was forced to pay an indemnity of 150 million francs, which crippled the economy of the fledgling republic. In addition, as the United States, a country where slavery had yet to be abolished, was threatened by the neighboring independent black republic to its south, and subsequently imposed some form of a trade embargo for nearly 100 years.[120]

Later, concern about German influence on Haiti's economy, as well as President Guillaume Sam's hanging by an enraged crowd, led the United States to enter and occupy the country from 1915 until 1934. While the U.S. occupation brought about many benefits, such as structural reform and the development of infrastructure, it also led to significant urbanization and created the Haitian National Guard (FAd'H), which later became the Armée d'Haiti, which was responsible for mass atrocities against the people of Haiti. The occupation also produced a small elite that continued to dominate Haiti politically and economically with the support of foreign powers, including the United States and France. Once free of the foreign occupations of the 19th and early 20th centuries, Haiti faced internal domination from dictatorships under Dr. François "Papa Doc" Duvalier (1957-71) and his son, Jean-Claude "Baby Doc" Duvalier (1971-86). In 1986, tension against Baby Doc's notoriously corrupt regime heightened, leading him to flee into exile while a military *junta* took over the state. Outbursts of violence and a round of bloody military coups followed the departure of Jean-Claude Duvalier in February 1986 and lasted until the United Nations (UN)-sponsored election that brought Father Jean-Bertrand Aristide to power in December 1990. Aristide generated support among Haiti's poor majority, creating a wave of democratic hope. Although he received the majority vote of the Haitian people, his political party won few seats.

The expectations that accompanied the election of the first democratically elected president in Haitian history were raised—only to be unrealized. Despite the hope that becoming a democracy created, the election of Aristide threatened the Haitian elite, who historically had enjoyed political and economic dominance. Subsequently, Aristide faced resistance, including a coup attempt before even taking office in 1991. Shortly after becoming President, Aristide was deposed by a military coup that killed over 1,000 people in its first days and forced him into exile.[121] The former Commander in Chief of the Haitian Armed Forces, Lieutenant-General Raoul Cédras, took over and forcibly appointed an interim president. This led to Haiti's bloodiest coup, which claimed the lives of 1,500 people; 40,000 fled the country, and, according to a report by the United Nations Development Program, between 200,000 and 300,000 fled the capital to the countryside as General Cedras took over the government and forced Aristide into exile.[122] The years that followed were plagued with misrule, violence, and military-sponsored changes in the constitution, leaving little room for peace in the country.[123]

The new leadership under Joseph Narette was not recognized by the international community, which threw its support behind Aristide. The 3 years that followed were characterized by political turmoil, human rights violations, and mass migration.

POLITICAL VIOLENCE

Political violence has been a method of achieving and sustaining power by means of arbitrary arrests, detentions, torture, and the killing of citizens suspected of opposing the regime. The main perpetrators were civilian militias that were established to use as counterforces to opposition groups, as well as the national army—which has a legacy of overthrowing Haitian governments. Rule by terror was characteristic of the Duvalier regimes.[124] Yet, even with Haiti's first democratically elected President in power, political violence has continued.

With international pressure and a U.S.-led Multinational Force (MNF), Aristide was reinstated in 1994 and finished his term as President in 1996. At that time Aristide was unable to run for President due to a constitutional restriction limiting his rule to 5 years. In his place, President Preval, a close associate to Aristide, ruled from 1996-2000. Aristide was reelected in 2000.

Both supporters and opponents of Aristide have continued to affect politics and violence in Haiti. In 2004, armed gangs, former combatants, and civilian police seized the towns, gradually took control over most of the north, and threatened to enter Port-au-Prince. Opposition led by the gangs called for Aristide's resignation, which prompted his second departure from Haiti. Most of the violence in Haiti continues to be meted out by gangs in the dense urban areas, which has caused numerous operational and tactical problems for international security forces trying to maintain law and order within the poverty-stricken population, let alone assist with the reformation of the Haitian security sector.

CORRUPTION

Governance in Haiti has a history of being co-opted by political violence and endemic corruption. Haiti has been categorized as a predatory state in which the rich and elite prey upon the poor and disenfranchised to move their political agendas forward within the Haitian political landscape. Corruption in Haiti is witnessed through the illegal use of public funds, drug trafficking by government officials, electoral fraud, and bribery, as well as interference with the normal functioning of national institutions such as the police and judiciary. Political will for SSR in Haiti is consistently undermined by those seeking to maintain corruption for their own private gain.

A small group of elites control most of Haiti's wealth and political decisions. The absence of civic values has resulted in a lack of interest in the fate of the country for the large, poor majority, who are mostly female and, on average, young. There is a lack of trust and confidence in government institutions among the poor, as well as disinterest, or lack of understanding, in supporting a participatory political culture. It is possible that there is no support for this type of politics because Haitian politics traditionally have been used as a means for oppression. No political leader thus far has commanded the respect of all classes that is required for a discussion of how to help the entire country.[125]

CRIMINALITY

After the national army was disbanded by Aristide in 1995, the security of various nonpolitical and political organizations (including Aristide's party, Famni Lavalas) was carried out by groups of young, disenfranchised armed men who were easily incited to mete out violence in urban areas.

Committing crimes was a way of survival in a devastating socio-economic situation. There is a profound linkage between poverty and violence in Haiti. So, in early 2004, the armed gangs included Aristide supporters, former officials of the Lavalas government, unofficial pro-Aristide armed gangs, gangs involved in the 1991 coup against Aristide, former military, former police, and nonpolitical groups. Gang-on-gang violence over urban territory and kidnappings are habitual and contribute to Haiti's security reality. Feeding into this is a mass of unemployed and uneducated youth, drawn to the gangs as a source of livelihood. Gangs also stand in the midst of politics, ready to mobilize when windows of opportunity present themselves that benefit the elite by inciting riots and unrest.

Environment.

Haiti was once a lush tropical paradise. As recently as 1925, 60 percent of Haiti's original forest covered its land.[126] Now, however, Haiti is considered to be an ecological disaster. Many factors contributed to Haiti's environmental degradation, including deforestation, soil erosion, water shortages, urbanization, and demographic pressure. The most significant of these factors is deforestation, primarily for the purpose of cutting trees for charcoal, which reached a peak during the international embargoes in the 1990s. In addition, cutting trees and selling firewood is one of the few options, other than crime, for earning a living. Haiti lost 44 percent of its total forest between 1999 and 2000.[127] In 2008, only 1.5 percent of forested land remained.[128] As the forests were cut down for fuel and livelihood needs, the mountainous regions became much more vulnerable to the impacts of tropical storms and hurricanes. The rich topsoil washed down the hills and was deposited in rivers, lakes, and bays. As a result, farmers are progressively left with less fertile soil, and, when the storms are particularly severe, mudslides and floods threaten communities.[129] In addition to these issues, Haiti experienced an oil embargo, which meant that Haitians had to identify alternative fuel supplies, signalling the beginning of massive deforestation. The effects of the sanctions and embargo still reverberate in Haiti — politically, economically, and environmentally.

INTERNATIONAL INTERVENTIONS

With no fewer than six international interventions in Haiti and two multinational forces between 1993 and 2004,[130] there are several facets to international involvement contributing to Haiti's ongoing crises. In addition to these interventions, there have been ongoing interventions by international organizations (such as the Organization for American States [OAS]) and nongovernmental organizations (NGOs). Although the international community has been attempting to *stabilize* the failed state of Haiti, the enforcement of an embargo in 1991-94 and again in 2000, sanctions, international and donor policies, as well as the premature exiting of prior UN missions, have all caused major instability in the country.

Before 2004 the UN missions were largely considered to have exited Haiti prematurely, often interpreting an election as a goalpost to which democracy and stability would eventually take hold. Intervention in Haiti has followed a pattern of elections, a coup, an embargo, further destabilization, and a cycle of intervention. It was not until United Nations Stabilization Mission in Haiti (MINUSTAH) that the international community recognized that a long-term commitment was needed to secure Haiti's future.

HAITI TIMELINE[131]

January 1, 1804. Haiti gains independence from France.
1807-20. Civil war between north and south Haiti.
1821-44. Haiti invades and occupies Santo Domingo (Dominican Republic from 1844).
1915-34. The United States invades and occupies Haiti.

1957. Dr. François "Papa Doc" Duvalier is elected President through military-controlled elections.

1959. Duvalier creates his private militia (Tontons Macoutes), following an attempted coup.

1964. Duvalier proclaims himself President-for-Life.

1971. Papa Doc Duvalier dies in office after naming his 19 year-old son Jean-Claude ("Baby Doc") as his successor.

February 7, 1986. Jean-Claude Duvalier leaves Haiti following popular unrest and external pressure.

1986-1990. Succession of military coups.

December 16, 1990. Father Jean-Bertrand Aristide is elected President with 67.5 percent of the votes in Haiti's first-ever democratic election.

September 30, 1991. Military coup by General Raoul Cedras. Aristide goes into exile. An international embargo is imposed against Haiti in October 1991.

September 19, 1994. A United States-led military intervention leads to the return of President Aristide in October.

April 28, 1995. Aristide abolishes the National Army.

1996-2000. As Aristide is not eligible for a second consecutive term, René Préval, a close associate, is elected President.

November 29, 2000. Aristide is elected President in an election marked by fraud and extremely low participation. Economic sanctions are imposed on Haiti.

January-February 2004. Haiti celebrates 200 years of independence. Celebrations marred by violence denouncing President Aristide. Aristide is forced into exile; interim government takes over.

February 29, 2004. The Security Council authorizes the deployment of a Multinational Interim Force to be followed by the United Nations Stabilization Mission in Haiti (MINUSTAH).

March 17, 2004. A Government of Transition is formed under Prime Minister Gerard Latortue.

May 2004. 2,000 die or disappear following severe floods in the south and in parts of the Dominican Republic.

June 2004. UN peacekeepers arrive take over U.S.-led multinational force.

September 2004. 3,000 die due to flooding in the north, in the wake of tropical storm Jeanne.

Late 2004. Haiti witnesses a rise in the levels of political and gang violence in the capital. Armed gangs loyal to former President Aristide are believed to be responsible for numerous killings.

July 2005. At least 45 people die following Hurricane Dennis.

February 2006. Rene Préval becomes President in the first general elections since former President Aristide was ousted in 2004.

June 2006. Prime Minister Jacques-Édouard Alexis takes office.

September 2006. The UN launches a program to disarm gang members in return for grants and job training.

January 2007. UN troops launch robust offensive against armed gangs in Cité Soleil.

October 2007. The UN Security Council extends the UN peacekeeping mission in Haiti for a year, noting significant improvements in security in recent months but saying the situation remains fragile.

April 2008. Riots break out over the rising price of food. The Government announces an emergency plan to cut price of rice in bid to halt unrest. Prime Minister Alexis is dismissed by Parliament.

May 2008. Brazil increases its peacekeeping force to help combat wave of kidnappings-for-ransom.

August-September 2008. Haiti is hit by four devastating hurricanes. More than 1,000 people were killed or have gone missing, and hundreds are left injured.

October 2008. UN Security Council passes resolution 1840 extending the UN mission for another year, with the intention of further renewal, stating that despite progress achieved thus far, the situation in Haiti continues to be a threat to international peace and security in the region.

UNITED NATIONS STABILIZATION MISSION IN HAITI (MINUSTAH)

According to a United Nations Development Programme report, "the numerous United Nations Missions that preceded MINUSTAH were rather limited in scope, addressing essentially the creation of a police force. They also suffered from the well-known weakness of such missions, their limited time horizons. In contrast, the mandate given to MINUSTAH in 2004 was much broader."[132]

Creating a secure and stable environment was first mandated in Security Council Resolution 1542, which authorized the deployment of MINUSTAH in 2004 with the mission's short-term goal aimed at creating a sufficiently stable environment so as to allow democratic elections to take place.[133] The long-term goals included the strengthening of capacities of the Haitian Government through stipulating that the mission should "assist the transitional government in monitoring, restructuring, and reforming the Haitian National Police . . .", "assist the transitional government, particularly the Haitian National Police with a comprehensive and sustainable Disarmament, Demobilization, and Reintegration program for all groups...", and "assist the restoration and maintenance of the rule of law . . . including the re-establishment of the prison system."[134]

Security Council Resolution 1702 (2006) included the expansion of SSR:

1. the number of police officers increased to 1,951;

2. 16 corrections officers were authorized for deployment;

3. the mission reoriented its DDR efforts toward a comprehensive community violence program; assisted with the restructuring and maintenance of the rule of law, public safety, and public order; was to provide assistance and advice to the Haitian authorities, in consultation with relevant actors, in monitoring, restructuring, reforming, and strengthening of the justice sector, including through technical assistance to review all relevant legislation; the provision of experts to serve as professional resources; the rapid identification and implementation of mechanisms to address prison overcrowding and prolonged pretrial detention, and the coordination and planning of these activities.[135]

With the extension of the mandate through Security Council Resolution 1780 (2007), another expansion of SSR was established. Although there was no explicit mention of SSR, there were the beginning signs of more integrated approaches to security and development.

The additions to the mandate were:

1. an increase in military and police composition, to 7,060 and 2,091;

2. provision of technical expertise in support of a comprehensive border management approach;

3. a request for UN Country Team and all relevant humanitarian actors to compliment security operations; and,

4. a request for the continuation of the community violence reduction approach, including through the National Commission on Disarmament, Dismantlement, and Reintegration.

Security Council Resolution 1840 (2008) addressed the components of security sector reform by focusing on:

1. Haitian National Police (HNP) reform;

2. land and maritime border management;

3. rule of law institutions; and,

4. MINUSTAH's community violence reduction approach.

Alongside a more comprehensive security sector focus, was the Security Council's decision to maintain current levels of troops and police officers at the current configuration of up to 7,060 and 2,091. The maintenance of that configuration follows from the Secretary General's recommendation to maintain the composition until "the planned and substantial increase of the [HNP] capacity allows for a reassessment of the situation. . . ."[136]

MINUSTAH and the UN have a key role to play in SSR, and the subsequent Security Council mandates have reflected this in successively reinforcing and expanding SSR activities.

SECURITY SECTOR REFORM IN HAITI

SSR in Haiti is aimed at enabling an environment that is conducive to development, democracy, peace, and security. Progress in SSR has not yet reached a threshold where a minimum standard of security and stability can be sustained. In this regard, SSR has been unsuccessful in the absence of a comprehensive strategy: it lacks resources, does not hold the confidence of the population, and lacks coherence among international and national actors. This reality was most recently exposed in the April 2008 protests and riots, which demonstrated that spoilers in Haiti still have the capacity to manipulate the discontented population, and revealed the government's incapacity to react to and dispel the riots. There are increasing calls by the international community for swift and decisive improvement to the reform process.[137]

In Haiti, SSR has focused on the HNP and judicial and prison reform, as well as DDR activities. Of less relevance have been the military, customs, border guards, coast guards, and parliamentary reforms.[138]

Haitian National Police (HNP).

Prior to 1994, Haitian police functions, as well as the prison system, were under the authority of the Haitian armed forces. At that time, the police force was a mechanism to mete out violence and repression in which the military had been engaged. Since this period, a decision was made to create a new independent and professional police force, and after the disbandment of the national army under Aristide, the HNP became the only security and law enforcement institution available to Haiti. The international community has been very active in building the capacity of the police through a process of professionalization. After that of the United Nations Mission in Kosovo, this is the second largest civilian police component of any of the 15 active UN peacekeeping missions.[139]

The tension between policing and militarism exists in Haiti, and is manifesting itself between the HNP and the political forces wishing to reconstitute the Haitian army. Both are sensitive and divisive issues and, if neglected, have the potential to have destabilizing long-term rule of law effects. Since the disbanding of the Haitian army in 1995, the HNP remains the cornerstone of security in Haiti, as it is the only institution that can apply and enforce the law.

The creation of a professional police force was the centerpiece of the U.S.-led MNF in the mid-1990s. Yet, any progress in creating a professional force was quickly lost with a series of events beginning with the ousting of former President Aristide in 2001 by a military coup and with the disengagement of the international community. At this time, the HNP became involved in the political conflict and became widely considered as a corrupt and illegitimate force.[140] With the deployment of MINUSTAH in 2004, it took nearly 2 years for the reform process to begin to take hold. Since then, police reform and vetting have steadily moved forward, a process that is largely attributed to the political space created by President Preval upon taking office.[141]

The HNP faces several challenges in its relations with the Haitian people, it is accused of brutality, human rights abuses, corruption, and involvement with politicians and criminal activity. Overall, there is a high degree of mistrust toward the HNP. These challenges are magnified by the fact that security and stability have not been consolidated, even after decades of international intervention. Some have claimed that there is a need for a second force in Haiti, either a new Haitian Armed Forces or a gendarmerie. The belief that a second force is required is grounded in the argument that the HNP does not have the capacity to protect the people against armed gangs and does not have the ability to protect borders, particularly against narco-traffickers.[142] Such an armed force could act as a counterweight to the HNP, which is composed of ex-military and armed gang remnants who have vested self-interests. Over 800 ex-soldiers make up the HNP ranks, particularly the high ranks. It is important to remember that these former combatants were highly abusive at the height of their activity and helped destabilize the rule of law. Any reinstatement of their regime would further undermine the levels of trust between Haitians and the security sector.[143] Many consider that the reestablishment of an army would constitute a threat to the coherence of the security sector, and would also serve as an expensive duplication of other established security forces. Further, if the formation of an HNP specialized border protection unit is realized, there will be no need for a military-type force. This type of HNP specialization is under discussion.

Moreover, the FAd'H was notorious for its brutality, and Haitians are fearful of its reestablishment.[144] Currently, the greatest proponent of reinstating the army, a former FAd'H colonel, Senator Youri Latortue, has prompted Preval to create the Presidential Commission for Reflection on National Security.[145] The commission is responsible for creating a comprehensive security strategy, which is forthcoming.

Despite over a decade of international community support, the HNP remains in a reform process directed through MINUSTAH. The number of police officers is still short of the ideal number for the maintenance of the rule of law and to protect a population of over eight million people. The police force suffers from a negative public image in Port-au-Prince, and it is commonly assumed that the force itself is corrupt. This opinion exists in lesser degrees in rural areas.

Although progress in SSR has been slow, the international community is increasingly calling for swift and decisive improvement to the reform process. MINUSTAH and the UN have a key role to play in SSR, and the successive Security Council mandates have reflected this in successively reinforcing and expanding SSR activities.

CHALLENGES TO SECURITY SECTOR REFORM

Comprehensive Strategy for SSR.

In Haiti, there has been no vision of a holistic SSR. Rather, the approach has been a compartmentalized one, not appreciating the interconnectedness of all of the actors' activities. The international community's stove-piped approach ignores how each sector is interconnected, which has negative results when the failure of one often leads to the failure of the whole. SSR requires the balanced realization of all its components, particularly in light of the links among poverty, lack of development, and violence. SSR initially suffered from a misdiagnosis of the situation, in that Haiti was treated as a traditional post-conflict country. Haiti is not at war, but nor is it a post-conflict situation, rather, it is experiencing a violent, protracted transition. The questionable conceptualization of a post-conflict situation has led to inappropriate elements being introduced into the mission's mandate, such as DDR activities. The consequences of a lack of context-specific strategy are most visible in Haiti's prolonged problem with groups who have not been disarmed, particularly ex-FAd'H.

The international community in Haiti has failed to harness the linkages between security and development in its planning and implementation of SSR. As a result, Haiti has not established a balance among the components of the security sector. For example, the Haitian judicial and correctional systems remain in a state of failure.

Coordination, cooperation, and communication of SSR activities within the mission, as well as with other UN agencies, donors, and locals is critical to ensure that resources are placed where they are needed most for effective implementation, local ownership, and to avoid duplication. Cooperation and coordination of SSR activities has met with problems in all sectors of SSR, which has contributed to delayed reform. Although there are in several cases structures in place to guarantee coordination and cooperation, in practice they have not functioned adequately.[146]

Resources.

The capacity to fully conduct and implement SSR has been lacking throughout the mission. This is due to a combination of factors, among them the inability to get the required number of people as mandated in the resolutions to the mission—meaning that posts, often at high levels, have remained empty for considerable periods of time—and securing people with the necessary skill sets to conduct reform. Overall, the mission has suffered from the problem that all French-speaking missions do: a lack of French speaking capacity.

Public Confidence.

Although MINUSTAH has the legitimacy of operating under Security Council Mandate 1542, the international presence is mostly met with dissatisfaction, distrust, and often outright resistance from the Haitian population. To many Haitians, MINUSTAH has not been seen as a neutral force. MINUSTAH is also met with disdain for its implication in human rights abuses as well as its inability to bring improvements to the lives of average Haitians despite years of intervention. This negative image is reinforced by the perception that there has been minimal communication between MINUSTAH and the population and a lack of transparency. To deal with these problems, SSR activities will have to integrate extensive consultation and implementation with locals and civil society.

Gender.

In Haiti, there continues to be a prevalence of violence against women who have little recourse to obtain justice for crimes committed against them, and are often met with disdain or they risk being physically abused if they attempt to complain or report crimes. Since Haitian women and girls have been most affected by the violent social upheaval, special attention is required in order to create an environment conducive to the promotion of their rights. MINUSTAH's gender unit has a twofold mandate: (1) to advise mission components on integrating a gender perspective throughout all of the programs and activities undertaken by MINUSTAH (DDR, police, human rights, etc.); and (2) to advise mission leaders in cooperation with civil society, including women's groups, in order to build capacities for local ownership of the transformation of their society.[147]

The Gender Unit has been involved in training the HNP as well as in train-the-trainer courses, mostly focusing on mainstreaming gender throughout the force, with particular emphasis on preventing violence against women. There are proposals to institutionalize this training capacity within the police academy. Also, UNPOL has gender focal points throughout the country, which visit prisons and police stations to ensure women are fairly and properly treated and separated, as well as accompany women to police stations if they wish to report a crime or make a complaint. The Gender Unit is also involved in DDR activities, though limited. An example of such involvement is the promotion of women's engagement in conflict resolution as agents of change within their communities.[148]

HAITI POLICING AND LAW ENFORCEMENT

According to the *Implementing Security Sector Reform* report co-published by the Center for Naval Analyses and Peacekeeping and Stability Operations Institute in 2008,[149] interventions—in particular stability operations—are pursued because the rule of law is not operating in a host nation. In the case of Haiti, there was indeed a rule of law framework at work in the country, however, it was one that was unacceptable to the community of international states and actors. Haiti has vacillated between a permissive and nonpermissive environment, which has made some of the SSR activities an ongoing challenge.

Based on the nature of the environment—permissive and nonpermissive—in which reform activities occur, policing activities will differ in important ways. In a permissive environment, policing should focus on law enforcement underpinned by traditional police techniques, such as investigation and community policing. In a nonpermissive environment, policing must be extended to include a paramilitary element focused on responding to gangs and insurgent violence. This will help strengthen the rule of law and enforce a semblance of human security for a country's population.

In both permissive and nonpermissive environments, building police capacity requires an integrated effort to be effective. This effort must encompass individual and collective training and long-term mentorship of police forces; establishment of effective support (including salary payment and logistics) for those forces; and the development of legitimate host nation senior leaders in the law enforcement sector. Moreover, police training is best accomplished by specialized knowledgeable trainers.

In a permissive environment, building police capacity should focus on classic police training in law enforcement techniques. In a nonpermissive environment, if the host nation requires a *paramilitary stability police force*,[150] then military training will be required for those forces. Some of the countries that contribute to MINUSTAH SSR activities do not have national capacities for this type of policing (i.e., Canada and the United States) and need to rely upon bilateral partners who have paramilitary police forces (i.e., Italy and France) for structuring, equipping, and training that capability.

Adequate resourcing to build police capacities in Haiti must become a sustained focus of SSR policing programs. Police training is resource intensive, and programs must provide sufficient technical trainers and police advisors to raise host nation policing capacity to levels required for transition within the projected transition time frame. Funding for police capacity building should be projected at $12 million per 1,000 police trained, and adequate funding levels must be established and maintained until requisite host nation capacity is achieved.[151]

Police training is not enough in Haiti to adequately address systemic policing issues, including law enforcement. If HNP are to be effective, they need to be provided with appropriate support when inserted back into the local environment. At a minimum, support must include adequate enabling logistics and a robust police advisor effort. This is especially true when returning to duties in the large urban centers, which are recognized for their absence of the rule of law. In nonpermissive environments, direct military support and operational collaboration between police and military units is required to enable host nation police operations. Military and law enforcement planners should incorporate that requirement into stabilization planning models.

In Haiti's nonpermissive urban environment, determining whether the police are being targeted is critical in the SSR assessment phase, and assessment models should incorporate this as a fundamental task. SSR planning must include an appropriate concept of operations for police force protection in the event that Haitian police are deliberately targeted by combatant groups. In Haiti, a HNP force was planned from the beginning of the first intervention in the early 1990s. It is critical to determine what model will be followed in advance of operations and how it will be established in the early stages of SSR planning. In a sense, this has been a key component to developing the HNP, however, it has not secured a level of success as of yet.

Key questions to be answered in the SSR assessment process should include:

- Who hires the police?
- Who directs police operations?
- What is the relationship of the police to the national, provincial, and local power structures?

In Haiti, a national model is being utilized, and SSR activities include capacity building at the ministerial level and support for the development of relationships between the appropriate host nation ministries and local policing activities.

External actors continue to support, train, and/ or direct police activities in Haiti. Determining the appropriate role(s) for such actors in Haitian policing is critical and should be evaluated on an ongoing basis. Whatever the initial role(s), external involvement in Haitian policing will almost certainly change over time. SSR planning could shape that change to support progressively greater Haitian autonomy. Where external actors and the Haitian government exercise shared sovereignty in directing or controlling police operations, processes for the direction/control of police, including mentoring and *right-hand/seat* guidance, must be jointly developed and implemented.

HNP effectiveness could be assessed on a regular basis as SSR proceeds, with the most critical measure being the degree to which host nation communities rely on the police as the first responder of choice, rather than militias, external forces, or private security companies.

SUMMARY

Haiti's reality is understood through socio-economic devastation, criminality, a weak and corrupt government, a disenfranchised and frustrated population, and an uncertain future for the international intervention.[152] These realities continue to influence the MINUSTAH intervention, which was further affected by the 2008 food, fuel, and economic crises and the four hurricanes that hit Haiti the same year. All factors compound the fact that Haiti remains a failed state despite international interventions and robust SSR programming in support of the rule of law.

SSR efforts in Haiti have produced poor returns, with few gains made toward an environment conducive to development, democracy, peace, and security. Despite having spent hundreds of millions of dollars for intervention support dedicated to the reform of the Haitian security sector, strengthening the rule of law through policing and law enforcement remains elusive. Establishing a rule of law framework that conforms to international standards continues to demand much effort, time, and resources to create a fully functional rule of law process. It is important to note that it will take time for Haiti to adopt a fully functional and legitimate host nation rule of law framework, underwritten by the HNP and the enforcement of law in the chaotic urban environments on Haitian shores. Considering that Haiti remains a failed state marked by economic devastation, environmental degradation, gang warfare, egregious human rights violations, and abject poverty, it is difficult to estimate just how much time will be required to invest in Haiti to increase its resilience.

DISCUSSION QUESTIONS

1. Why is the state failure of Haiti a concern for the United States?

2. What is a predatory state? Describe how Haiti's political elites have designed state institutions to serve their political agendas.

3. Why do Haiti's urban centers lack the rule of law? Why is Port-au-Prince important to SSR planning and sustainable outcomes?

4. In what way has MINUSTAH built local capacities in the security sector to support policing and law enforcement in Haiti?

5. In your opinion, and compared against the tenets of accountability, transparency and effectiveness, have MINUSTAH's SSR activities in support of the HNP been successful for the future of Haiti as a resilient state in the Americas?

ADDITIONAL REFERENCES

United Nations Security Council Resolutions on Haiti.

United Nations Security Council Resolution 1542 (2004). *daccessdds.un.org/doc/UNDOC/GEN/N04/332/98/PDF/N0433298.pdf?OpenElement.*

United Nations Security Council Resolution 1840 (2008).*daccessdds.un.org/doc/UNDOC/GEN/ N08/548/96/PDF/N0854896.pdf?OpenElement.*

Reports and Publications.

Bazin, Marc. "Haiti Under Preval's Presidency: A Window of Opportunity?" September 25, 2008.

Bureau of Democracy, Human Rights and Labor, Government of Haiti. "2008 Human Rights Report: Haiti," February 25, 2009. *www.reliefweb.int/rw/ RWFiles2009.nsf/FilesByRWDocUnidFilename/LSGZ-7PMH47-full_report.pdf/$File/full_report.pdf.*

Country Indicators for Foreign Policy. "Democracy and Governance: Haiti," Fall 2007. *www.carleton.ca/ cifp/app/serve.php/1041.pdf* .

_____. "Fragile States Country Report No. 7: Haiti," September 2007. *www.carleton.ca/cifp/app/ serve.php/1123.pdf* .

_____. "Haiti: A Risk Assessment Brief," February 2009. *www.carleton.ca/cifp/app/serve.php/ 1210.pdf* .

Dziedzic, Michael, and Robert M. Perito. *Special Report - Haiti: Confronting the Gangs of Port-au-Prince.* Washington, DC: United States Institute for Peace, September 2008.

Faubert, Carrol. *Case Study Haiti: Evaluation of UNDP Assistance to Conflict-Affected Countries.* New York: United Nations Development Programme Evaluation Office, 2006.

Hanggi, Heiner, and Vicenza Sherrer. "Security Sector Reform and UN Integrated Missions: Experience from Burundi, the Democratic Republic of Congo, Haiti, and Kosovo." December 2007. *www.ssrnetwork.net/document_library/detail/4124/security-sector-reform-and-un-integrated-missions-experience-from-burundi-the-democratic-republic-of-congo-haiti-and-kosovo.*

Harvard University. "Keeping the Peace in Haiti?" March 31, 2005. *www.reliefweb.int/rw/RWFiles2005.nsf/FilesByRWDocUNIDFileName/VBOL-6B5J5U-harvard-haiti-mar05.pdf/$File/harvard-haiti-mar05.pdf.*

International Crisis Group. "Haiti 2009: Stability at Risk," *Latin America/Caribbean Briefing N°19,* March 3, 2009. *www.crisisgroup.org/home/index.cfm?id=5952&l=1.*

_____. "Haiti: Justice Reform and the Security Crisis," Latin America/Caribbean Briefing No. 14, Jan. 31, 2007. *www.crisisgroup.org/home/index.cfm?id=4639&l=1.*

_____. "Reforming Haiti's Security Sector," Latin America/Caribbean Report No. 28, September 18, 2008. *www.crisisgroup.org/home/index.cfm?id=5681&l=1.*

Mendelson-Forman, J. "Security Sector Reform in Haiti," *International Peacekeeping*, Vol. 13, No. 1, 2006, pp. 14-27. *www.ssrnetwork.net/document_library/detail/4151/security-sector-reform-in-haiti.*

Mobekk, Eirin. 'MINUSTAH and the Need for a Context-Specific Strategy: The Case of Haiti', in *Security Sector Reform and UN Integrated Missions: Experience from Burundi, the Democratic Republic of Congo, Haiti, and Kosovo*, H. Hanggi & V. Scherrer, eds. Geneva, Switzerland: DCAF, 2008, pp. 113-168.

Perito, Robert. "Haiti: Hope for the Future." June 2007. *www.usip.org/pubs/specialreports/sr188.html*.

Roc, Nancy. "Haiti – Environment: From the Pearl of Antilles to Desolation." September 2008. *ca.search. yahoo.com/search?ei=UTF-8&fr=hp-psnb&p=Haiti+% E2%80%93+Environment%3A+From+the+Pearl+of+ Antilles+to+Desolation*.

United Nations Secretary-General. "Report of the Secretary-General on Haiti (S/2004/300)," April 16, 2004. *www.peacekeepingbestpractices.unlb.org/PBPS/ Library/SG%20Report%20on%20Haiti%2016.04.04. pdf*.

_____. "Briefed on its fact-finding mission to Haiti, Security Council learns of prospects to ensure long-term political stability, achieve sustainable development there," March 19, 2009. *www.reliefweb.int/rw/rwb.nsf/db900sid/EGUA- 7QAQR4?OpenDocument&rc=2&cc=hti*.

_____. "Report of the Secretary-General on the United Nations Stabilization Mission in Haiti (S/2009/129)," March 12, 2009. *www.reliefweb.int/ rw/RWFiles2009.nsf/FilesByRWDocUnidFilename/ EGUA-7Q3RXH-full_report.pdf/$File/full_report.pdf*.

Weblinks.

United Nations. "United Nations Stabilization Mission in Haiti." *www.minustah.org/.*

United Nations Development Fund for Women. "Policy Briefing Paper: Gender Sensitive Police Reform in Post-Conflict Societies." October 2007. *www.unifem.org/attachments/products/Gender SensitivePoliceReform_PolicyBrief_2007_eng.pdf.*

ENDNOTES

1. Richard Hill, Jon Temin, and Lisa Pacholek, "Building Security Where There Is No Security," *Journal of Peacebuilding and Development*, Vol. 3, No. 2, pp. 38-52.

2. *Security Sector Reform*, Washington, DC: U.S. Agency for International Development, U.S. Department of Defense, and U.S. Department of State, available from *pdf.usaid.gov/pdf_docs/ PNADN788.pdf*, p. 4.

3. Edward Rees, *Security Sector Reform and Peace Operations: Improvisation and Confusion from the Field*, New York: United Nations Department of Peacekeeping Operations, March 2006, available from *doc.operationspaix.net/serv1/MINUK_best_practices_ Rees_2006-03_.pdf.*

4. *Security Sector Reform*, p. 5.

5. *Ibid.*, p. 8.

6. Rees.

7. *Field Manual* (FM) 3-07, *Stability Operations*, Washington, DC: Headquarters, Department of the Army, October 6, 2008, p. 6-1.

8. *Security System Reform and Governance: A DAC Reference Document*, Paris, France: Organisation for Economic Co-Operations and Development, 2005, available from *www.oecd.org/dataoecd/8/39/31785288.pdf*,

9. Heiner Hänggi, "UN Approaches to SSR—an Overview," *Developing a Security Sector Reform (SSR) Concept for the United Nations*, Proceedings of the Expert Workshop held in Bratislava, Slovakia, on July 7, 2006, Bratislava, Slovakia: Ministry Of Foreign Affairs of The Slovak Republic and Democratic Control of Armed Forces, 2006, p. 38.

10. *Security System Reform and Governance*.

11. Kim Traavik, *Opening Lecture: International and Security Affairs Centre*, 9th School of Security Sector Reform, Belgrade, Serbia, April 23, 2007, available from *www.norway-nato.org/news/230407.htm*.

12. "Global Facilitation Network for Security Sector Reform," *A Beginner's Guide to Security Sector Reform* (SSR), March 2007, p. 2, available from *www.peacewomen.org/resources/SSR/Gender&SSR.pdf*.

13. Hänggi, p. 37.

14. *Security Sector Reform*, p. 4.

15. *Ibid.*, p. 6-1.

16. *Ibid.*, p. 6-2.

17. *Ibid.*, p. 6-2.

18. *Contributions for International Peacekeeping Activities*, Washington, DC: U.S. Department of State, 2008, p. 99, available from *www.state.gov/documents/organization/79838.pdf*.

19. *Ibid.*, p. 99.

20. FM 3-07, p. 6-3.

21. *Security Sector Reform*, p. 8.

22. *Report on the question of the use of mercenaries as a means of violating human rights and impeding the exercise of the right of peoples to self-determination, submitted by the Special Rapporteur of the Commission on Human Rights*, New York: United Nations General Assembly, 54th Session, 2000.

23. *Security Sector Reform*, p. 8.

24. For a complete overview of security sector reform activities important to the U.S. Government, please refer to FM 3-07, pp. 6-10-6-22.

25. Stability operations are military and civilian activities conducted across the spectrum from peace to conflict to establish or maintain order in states and regions while advancing U.S. interests. See Department of Defense Directive 3000.05, November 28, 2005.

26. Stephen John Stedman, "Spoiler Problems in Peace Processes," *International Security*, Vol. 22, No. 2, Fall 1997, pp. 5-53.

27. *Discussion Paper: A Proposed Global Convention Prohibiting the International Transfer of Military Small Arms and Light Weapons to Nonstate Actors*, New York: Canadian Mission to the UN in New York, December 1998, available from *www.nisat.org/export_laws-regs%20linked/canada/discusion_papera_proposed.htm*.

28. This summary is based on the recommendations in "Implementing Security Sector Reform," *Security Sector Reform Workshop, Interim Report*, Thomas Dempsey, ed., Alexandria, VA: The Center for Naval Analyses, and Carlisle, PA: The Peacekeeping and Stability Operations Institute, December 4, 2008, available from *https://pksoi.army.mil/Docs/Governance/SSR_Workshop_Interim_Report.pdf*.

29. Glenn Ruga and Julie Mertus, *History of the War in Kosovo*, Lowell, MA: Center for Balkan Development, April 1999, available from *www.friendsofbosnia.org/edu_kos.html*.

30. This useful timeline is taken from BBC News online, BBC NEWS, *Kosovo Timeline*, BBC Online, December 9, 2008, available from *news.bbc.co.uk/go/pr/fr/-/1/hi/world/europe/country_profiles/3550401.stm*.

31. United Nations Security Council Resolution 1244, New York: United Nations, 1999.

32. *Kosovo's Fragile Transition*, Europe Report N.196, New York: International Crisis Group, September 25, 2008, available from *www.crisisgroup.org/home/index.cfm?id=5695&l=1*.

33. United Nations Development Programme, New York: United Nations, *www.ks.undp.org/?cid=2,1,59*.

34. *Kosovo's Fragile Transition*.

35. *Ibid.*

36. United Nations Security Council Resolution 1244.

37. *Ibid.*

38. *Report of the Secretary-General on the United Nations Interim Administration Mission in Kosovo,* S/1999/1250, New York: United Nations Security Council, December 23, 1999, p. 3.

39. *A Kosovo Roadmap (II): Internal Benchmarks*, Europe Report N.125, New York: International Crisis Group, March 1, 2002, available from www.crisisgroup.org/home/index.cfm?id=1687&l=1.

40. *Ibid.*

41. *Report of the Secretary-General on the United Nations Interim Administration Mission in Kosovo*, New York: United Nations Security Council, S/1999/1250, December 23, 1999. pp. 26-27.

42. UNMIK website, *Fact Sheet*, available from *www.unmikonline.org/docs/2008/Fact_Sheet_July_2008.pdf*.

43. KIPRED. Kosovo's Internal Security Sector Review: Stages I & II, Strategic Environment Review & Security Threats Analysis, March 2006, p. 6.

44. For example, although Timor Leste (East Timor) is usually touted as a successful UN peacekeeping mission since the mission inception in 1999, there were 22 UN Security Council Resolutions up until February 2009. These included 1236, 1246, 1257, 1262, 1264, 1272, 1319, 1338, 1392, 1410, 1473, 1480, 1543, 1573, 1599, 1677, 1690, 1704, 1703, 1745, 1802, and 1867. Although there is no substantiated correlation between the success of a mission and the number of UN Resolutions, the more unsuccessful missions — categorized by mission creep, cost, number of troops, and police compared to levels of security, etc. — appear to have more than their share of resolutions. Haiti is an excellent case to support this point.

45. "Implementing Security Sector Reform."

46. United Nations Security Council Resolution 1244.

47. KIPRED, p. 6.

48. *A Kosovo Roadmap (II)*

49. KIPRED, p. 9.

50. "Liberia: Uneven Progress in Security Sector Reform," Africa Report No. 48, New York: International Crisis Group, January 13, 2009, p. 3, available from *www.crisisgroup.org/home/index.cfm?id=5867&l=1.*

51. *Ibid.*

52. "Liberia—First Civil War—1989-1996," April 27, 2005, Global Security, available from *www.globalsecurity.org/military/world/war/liberia-1989.htm.*

53. "Liberia - UNOMIL Background," New York: United Nations, available from *www.un.org/Depts/dpko/dpko/co_mission/unomilFT.htm#SEPTEMBER.*

54. *Ibid.*

55. *Ibid.*

56. "United Nations Mission in Liberia (UNMIL): History," New York: United Nations Department of Peacekeeping Operations, available from *www.un.org/Depts/dpko/missions/unmil/*.

57. *Ibid.*

58. *Ibid.*

59. The actual numbers are debated, because it is believed that some civilians posed as former combatants to receive payment and training.

60. "Country Profile 2008: Liberia," London, UK: Economist Intelligence Unit, 2008, p. 18, available from *www.eiu.com/report_dl.asp?issue_id=1843610169&mode=pdf&rf=0*.

61. The actual number of demobilized former combatants is debated, because it is believed that some civilians posed as former combatants to receive transitional payments and training. See "Appendix D: Ex-combatant Reintegration and SSR," *Liberia: Uneven Progress in Security Sector Reform*, Africa Report N°148, New York: International Crisis Group, January 13, 2009, available from *www.crisisgroup.org/home/index.cfm?id=5867&l=1*.

62. United Nations Mission in Liberia (UNMIL), "UN Envoy Urges Liberians to Take a Stand Against All Forms of Violence," February 20, 2008, available from *www.reliefweb.int/rw/rwb.nsf/db900sid/ASAZ-7C3KBR?OpenDocument&query=un%20envoy%20urges%20liberians%20to%20take%20a%20stand%20against%20violence&cc=lbr*.

63. "Security Council Presidential Statement Emphasizes Security Sector Reform Essential Element of Post-Conflict Stabilization and Reconstruction," New York: UN Security Council, May 12, 2008, p. 16, available from *www.reliefweb.int/rw/rwb.nsf/db900sid/KKAA-7EL4WH?OpenDocument&query=sc/9327%20security%20sector%20reform*.

64. "Security Council Resolution 1836 (2008)," New York: UN Security Council, September 29, 2008, available from *www.reliefweb. int/rw/rwb.nsf/db900sid/VDUX-7JXQS2?OpenDocument&rc=1&c c=lbr.*

65. "Liberia: Uneven Progress in Security Sector Reform."

66. "Implementing Security Sector Reform."

67. Abu Sherif, "Reintegration of Female War-affected and Ex-combatants in Liberia," In *Conflict Trends*, ACCORD, Issue 3, 2008, p. 28, available from *www.accord.org.za/publications/conflict-trends/downloads/416-conflict-trends-20083.*

68. Keith Crane, David Gompert, Olga Oliker, K. Jack Riley, and Brooke Stearns, "Making Liberia Safe: Transformation of the National Security Sector," Monograph, Santa Monica, CA: RAND, 2007, available from *www.rand.org/pubs/monographs/2007/ RAND_MG529.pdf.*

69. "Appendix D: Ex-combatant Reintegration and SSR," *Liberia: Uneven Progress in Security Sector Reform*, Africa Report N°148, New York: International Crisis Group, January 13, 2009, available from *www.crisisgroup.org/home/index.cfm?id=5867&l=1.*

70. Thomas Jaye, "An Assessment Report on Security Sector Reform in Liberia," Monrovia, Liberia: Governance Reform Commission (GRC) of Liberia, September 23, 2006, p. 14, available from *www.kaiptc.org/_upload/general/Lib_Assess_Rep_on_SSR.pdf.*

71. "Liberia: Uneven Progress in Security Sector Reform."

72. "United Nations Development Assistance Framework for Liberia: 2008-2011," Draft, New York: United Nations Development Programme (UNDP), April 2007, p. 8, available from *www.undp.org/execbrd/word/UNDAF%20RMs/LIBERIA%20 UNDAF%20FINAL%20DRAFT%2014%20April.doc.*

73. "Country Profile 2008: Liberia," 2008.

74. According to Liberia's national youth policy established in 2005, youth are defined as being between 15 and 35 years of age.

75. "United Nations Development Assistance Framework for Liberia: 2008-2011," p. 13.

76. *Ibid.*

77. Sherif, p. 28.

78. Sandra Oder, "Moving Forward: Liberia's Achievements for Engendering Security Sector Reform," Pretoria, South Africa: Institute for Security Studies, September 22, 2008, available from *www.iss.co.za/static/templates/tmpl_html.php?node_id=3623&slink_id=6585&slink_type=12&link_id=5.*

79. "Liberia: Poverty Reduction Strategy Paper," International Monetary Fund Country Report No. 08/219, Monrovia, Republic of Liberia: July 2008, available from *www.imf.org/external/pubs/ft/scr/2008.cr08219.pdf.*

80. Bruce Baker, "Post-war Policing by Communities in Sierra Leone, Liberia, Rwanda," in *Democracy and Security*, Vol. 3, No. 2, 2007, p. 12, available from *www.ssrnetwork.net/upload_files/3690.pdf.*

81. "United Nations Peace Operations: Year in Review," New York: United Nations Department of Peacekeeping Operations, 2008, available from *www.un.org/Depts/dpko/dpko/pub/yir2008.pdf.*

82. *Ibid.*

83. *Ibid.*

84. Mark Malan, "Security Sector Reform in Liberia: Mixed Results from Humble Beginnings," Carlisle, PA: Strategic Studies Institute, U.S. Army War College, 2008, available from *www.strategicstudiesinstitute.army.mil/pdffiles/pub855.pdf.*

85. "Country Profile 2008: Liberia."

86. "Liberia: As Armed Robbery Rises Civilians Defend Themselves," New York: Integrated Regional Information Networks, May 7, 2008, available from *www.reliefweb.int/rw/*

rwb.nsf/db900sid/MUMA-7EF522?OpenDocument&query=as%20 armed%20robbery%20rises%20civilians%20defend&cc=lbr.

87. Baker, p. 25.

88. "UN Envoy Urges Liberian Police to Serve the Interest of All, and Not Some, Liberians," New York: UN Mission in Liberia, June 12, 2008.

89. Based on 2006 data found in "At a Glance: Liberia," New York: UNICEF, 2009, available from *www.unicef.org/infobycountry/ liberia_statistics.html*.

90. "Liberia: As Armed Robbery Rises Civilians Defend Themselves."

91. "United Nations Peace Operations: Year in Review."

92. "Liberia: Uneven Progress in Security Sector Reform," p. 4.

93. Malan.

94. *Ibid.*

95. Baker, p. 12.

96. *Ibid.*

97. *Ibid*, p. 7.

98. *Ibid*, p. 8.

99. *Ibid*, pp. 8-10.

100. *Ibid*, p. 10.

101. *Ibid*, p. 15.

102. *Ibid.*

103. *Ibid*, p. 13.

104. *Ibid*.

105. *Ibid*, p. 16.

106. *Ibid*.

107. "Liberia: As Armed Robbery Rises Civilians Defend Themselves."

108. Baker, p. 16.

109. *Ibid*, pp. 18-19.

110. *Ibid*, p. 21.

111. *Ibid*, pp. 26, 23.

112. *Ibid*, p. 20.

113. *Ibid*, p. 23.

114. *Ibid*, pp. 20-21.

115. *Ibid*, p. 25.

116. *Ibid*, p. 23.

117. "UN Envoy Urges Liberians to Take a Stand Against All Forms of Violence."

118. *Ibid*.

119. *Ibid*.

120. Carlo Dade and John W. Graham, "The Role for Canada and Post-Aristide Haiti: Structures, Options and Leadership," April 2004, available from *www.focal.ca/ pdf/Haiti _post_aristide. pdf*.

121. Ambassade d'Haiti, "Key Dates in Haiti's History," available from *www.haiti.org/keydate.htm*.

122. Carrol Faubert, *Haiti Case Study: Evaluation of UNDP Assistance to Conflict-Affected Countries*, New York: United Nations Development Programme Evaluation Office, 2006, p. 9.

123. Major General Indar Rikhye, *The Politics and Practices of United Nations Peacekeeping: Past, Present and Future*, Toronto, Canada: Brown Book Company, 2000, p. 55.

124. The most notorious of the militias were Duvalier's *Tontons Macoutes* and Aristide's *Chimeres*.

125. Freedom House, *Countries at the Crossroads 2004 – Haiti 2004*, Online, United Nations, UNHCR Refworld, 2004, available from *unhcr.org/refworld/docid/473868f064.html*.

126. Philip Howard, "Environmental Scarcity and Conflict in Haiti: Ecology and Grievances in Haiti's Troubled Past and Uncertain Future," Ottawa Canada: Canadian International Development Agency, 1998, available from *faculty.washington.edu/ pnhoward/publishing/articles/haiti.pdf*.

127. Nancy Roc, "Haiti—Environment: From the Pearl of Antilles to Desolation," FRIDE: Comment September 2008, available from *ca.search.yahoo.com/search?ei=UTF-8&fr=hp-psnb& p=Haiti+%E2%80%93+Environment%3A+From+the+Pearl+of+Ant illes+to+Desolation*.

128. *Ibid.*

129. *From Conflict to Peacebuilding: The Role of Natural Resources and the Environment*, Nairobi, Kenya: United Nations Environment Programme, February 2009.

130. MINUSTAH website, available from *www.un.org/Depts/ dpko/missions/minustah/*.

131. British Broadcasting Corporation, "Haiti Timeline," available from *news.bbc.co.uk/2/hi/americas/1202857.stm*.

132. Faubert, p. 17.

133. "Peace Operations Fact Sheet Series: MINUSTAH, The United Nations Stabilization Mission in Haiti," Washington, DC: The Henry L. Stimson Center, July 16, 2008.

134. Security Council Resolution 1542, New York: United Nations Security Council, 2004.

135. Security Council Resolution 1720, New York: United Nations Security Council, 2006.

136. Security Council Resolution 1840, New York: United Nations Security Council, 2008.

137. "Haiti 2009: Stability at Risk," *Latin America/Caribbean Briefing No. 19*, New York: International Crisis Group, March 3, 2009, available from *www.crisisgroup.org/home/index.cfm?id=5952&1=1*.

138. Eirin Mobekk, "MINUSTAH and the Need for a Context-Specific Strategy: The Case of Haiti," Heiner Hanggi and Vicenza Sherrer, eds., *Security Sector Reform and UN Integrated Missions: Experience from Burundi, the Democratic Republic of Congo, Haiti, and Kosovo*, Geneva, Switzerland: Democratic Control of Armed Forces, 2008, p. pp. 113-168.

139. Faubert, p. 19.

140. *Keeping the Peace in Haiti?: An Assessment of the United Nations Stabilization Mission in Haiti Using Compliance with its Prescribed Mandate as a Barometer for Success*, Cambridge, MA, Rio de Janiero and São Paulo, Brazil: Centro de Justiça Global, and Harvard Law Student Advocates for Human Rights, March 2005, available from *www.law.harvard.edu/programs/hrp/documents/haitireport.pdf*.

141. "Reforming Haiti's Security Sector," *Latin America/Caribbean Report No. 28*, New York: International Crisis Group, September 18, 2008, available from *www.crisisgroup.org/home/index.cfm?id=5681&1*.

142. Amelie Gauthier, "Haiti: Voices of the Actors: A Research Project on the UN Mission," *FRIDE Working Paper*, February 15, 2008, available from *www.fride.org/publication/361/haiti-voices-of-the-actors-a-research-project-on-the-un-mission*.

112

143. Faubert, p. 14.

144. *Ibid.*

145. "Haiti 2009: Stability at Risk."

146. *Ibid.*

147. Nadine Puechguirbal, "Haiti: Putting Gender and Peacekeeping into Practice," *Focal Point*, Vol. 6, Issue 9, November 2007, available from *www.focal.ca/publications/focalpoint/fp1107/?article=article2&lang=f.*

148. Heiner Hanggi and Vicenza Sherrer, "Security Sector Reform and UN Integrated Missions: Experience from Burundi, the Democratic Republic of Congo, Haiti, and Kosovo," available from *www.ssrnetwork.net/document_library/detail/4124/security-sector-reform-and-un-integrated-missions-experience-from-burundi-the-democratic-republic-of-congo-haiti-and-kosovo.*

149. "Implementing Security Sector Reform."

150. The United States refers to paramilitary police as Stability Police, whereas the internationally community refers to these police as Formed Police Units (FPU). Some examples of national paramilitary police are the *Arma dei Carabinieri* (Italy), and the *Gendarmerie* (France). There is no equivalent of Stability Police or FPU in the United States or Canada.

151. Dempsey.

152. Mobekk, pp. 113-168.